IN DEFENCE OF LANDSCAPE

AN ARCHAEOLOGY OF PORTON DOWN

IN DEFENCE OF LANDSCAPE

AN ARCHAEOLOGY OF PORTON DOWN

DAVID RIDE

TEMPUS

First published 2006

Tempus Publishing Limited
The Mill, Brimscombe Port,
Stroud, Gloucestershire, GL5 2QG
www.tempus-publishing.com

British Library Cataloguing in Publication Data.
A catalogue record for this book is available from the British Library.

ISBN 0 7524 3749 6

Typesetting and origination by Tempus Publishing Limited
Printed in Great Britain

Contents

Foreword

By Dr Richard Scott, Programme Director Science and Technology (DSTL)

On 22 April 1915, the Germans used chemical weapons against the Allied forces for the first time. There became a requirement for a defensive and retaliatory UK capability, and in response to this the 'War Department Experimental Ground' was established. The Trench Warfare Scientific Advisory Committee visited a number of potential sites in southern England, but chose the 2,750 hectare site at Porton Down as the ideal location for field trials, given its shape, size and the predominant wind direction. The development of Porton Down as a chemical and biological research facility is well documented. David Ride explores the archaeology of this special landscape through the ages, from Neolithic remains to rather more recent, but equally interesting, gas trenches from the First World War.

Over the years MoD occupancy has protected Porton Down from the impact of modern agriculture, and it now serves as a reminder of a landscape that has otherwise disappeared from southern Britain. Conservation of this rare habitat has gained increasing importance, and much of Porton Down is now a Site of Special Scientific Interest (SSSI). Porton Down is also designated a Special Protection Area (SPA) for birds under the Birds Directive (1979), and is a proposed candidate for becoming a Special Area of Conservation (SAC) under the Habitats Directive (1992). The chalk grassland is home to an abundant mixture of flora and fauna, including a wide range of butterflies, over 20 species of ant, the rare stone curlew and a wide variety of chalk grassland plants. Juniper flourishes on the chalk and limestone soil, with about 20 percent of the UK's juniper found within the 7,000 acres of Porton Down, along with 15 of the 19 species of invertebrate specific to the shrub.

The Defence Science and Technology Laboratory (DSTL, part of the UK MoD) now occupies the site at Porton Down. The range at Porton is still used for chemical and biological defence trialling and increasingly for other defence-related trials. DSTL conducts these activities so as to maintain the unique landscape and the biodiversity that continues to increase, through careful management and liaison with key stakeholders.

In addition to environmental conservation, the MoD recognises the importance of the archaeology in its care. Metal stars on posts have long been a part of the military training landscape, denoting points of archaeological interest, and serving as a marker to prevent damage during exercises. Defence Estates employs a team of archaeologists to provide advice on all archaeological matters. The team contributes to the Army Training Estate's Integrated Rural Management Plan (IRMP), and offers advice on individual monument management. The MoD is committed to maintaining, protecting, and, where possible, enhancing the cultural heritage value of the Defence Estate. The MoD ensures that it complies with statutory obligations, procedures and guidance relating to designated cultural heritage sites. It works closely with the Statutory Bodies and other stakeholders to identify land of cultural heritage significance.

Porton Down's relationship with one of these bodies is longstanding. John Musty, a Porton Down scientist and amateur archaeologist, like David Ride, went on to head the Ministry of Works (now English Heritage) Ancient Monuments Laboratory. He is often credited with inventing the term 'archaeological science'. John Musty sadly died in 2000, but he would have been delighted that a tradition that he started at Porton is being carried on with such enthusiasm and rigour by David Ride.

Acknowledgements

It was David Field of English Heritage, always highly supportive of my archaeological work at Porton Down, who first suggested that the site merited a volume of its own and encouraged me to produce it. My thanks go to Peter Kemmis Betty of Tempus Publishing for accepting the project. Roy Canham, Wiltshire's County Archaeologist, always helpful with archaeological endeavours at Porton Down over many years, has written the Preface.

Dr Keith Norris, the Archivist and Vice President of the Bourne Valley Historical Society, provided a major input to this volume. His excellent but unpublished biography of Dr J.F.S. Stone, the archaeologist, forms the basis of Chapter 2; his work on the early history of Porton Down and research into dew-ponds and the Porton Light Railway has proved invaluable. Peter Hopson of the British Geological Survey taught me the geology of the Porton Down Range in three days of vigorous surveying; Peter also corrected my geological comments in this work. Mark Rigg provided information on steam ploughing. Staff of the National Monuments Record (English Heritage), Salisbury Reference Library, Trowbridge Reference Library, the Wiltshire and Swindon Record Office, and the University of Winchester have been most helpful.

Peter Saunders, Director of Salisbury and South Wiltshire Museum ('Salisbury Museum'), and David Algar, allowed and assisted me to photograph artefacts from their collections; I am grateful to them and the Trustees. I am indebted to the management of the Defence Science and Technical Laboratory (DSTL), Porton Down, for their cooperation in producing this book and for permission to publish visual material in their possession. Stuart Corbett, Conservation Officer at Porton Down, aided access to documents and photographs. Others who provided or located photographs, or helped with visual material, are Frank Blewett, Damian Grady, Michael Harvey, John Jochimsen, Barbara Last, Keith Norris, John Sheail, Barbara Watson, David Sutcliffe and Alan Winstanley. Dr John Chandler, co-editor of the magazine of the Wiltshire Archaeological and Natural History Society (WANHM), arranged agreement with the trustees to publish material from past volumes. Dr H.M. Darlow gave permission to publish from Dr Stone's second excavation notebook. All illustrations are individually credited except those that are mine.

David Field read and commented constructively on the early chapters, although we disagree about certain aspects of interpretation of the Bronze and Iron Ages; the opinions recorded in this book are my own. Graham Brown reviewed the chapter on sheep. Dr Ann Woodward reviewed my account of her work on Thorney Down. Richard Garston kindly proof read the manuscript and made helpful suggestions for its improvement.

The members of Porton Down's Conservation Group's Archaeological Section have worked tirelessly on sometimes difficult excavations. My wife, Sandra, is one of these; she has been unfailingly supportive of me during the writing of this work and has helped with the manuscript.

All these people, and many more, have earned my gratitude and thanks, which I am pleased to give in full measure, for their assistance and interest in this project.

David Ride

Preface

A glance at the geological map of southern Britain reveals a great central block of chalk land stretching some 40 miles from Warminster on the western borders of Wiltshire to Basingstoke in north Hampshire. The western half of this entity – Salisbury Plain – combines with its eastern component – the chalk uplands of northern Hampshire – to form a zone critical in the early development of southern England, attracting wave after wave of prehistoric settlement and colonisation.

In Wiltshire, the late nineteenth-century acquisition of Salisbury Plain Training Area by the then Office of War removed a large slice of this territory from the environmental ravages of the twentieth century, dedicating it to the surprisingly less harmful processes of military training. To the east of this block a similar stretch of untouched and undeveloped chalk downland located just a little to the north of the city of Salisbury, and at the very centre of the chalk land mass, was similarly favoured by an acquisition designed to serve a nation's need in times of stress – and this site is Porton Down. In both cases – Salisbury Plain and Porton Down – subsequent protection from environmental damage was a by-product of the intended use, and whereas the army estate on Salisbury Plain has carried the load of live artillery firing and armoured exercise, Porton has had little or none of this. It remains to this day an environmental gem, an outstanding historic landscape celebrated in the pages that follow by David Ride who has led the archaeological efforts of its superb conservation group for some 17 years.

As an untouched and undeveloped chalk land remnant, Porton is a happy hunting ground for the keen archaeologist. In his text, David explores the downland heritage, an unfolding of the history and development of our early societies captured in the detailed excavation of Neolithic flint mines, the remarkable heritage of Bronze Age burial mounds scattered across the Porton estate and the evidence of early Bronze Age settlement painstakingly acquired in the fastidious excavations of J.F.S. Stone. To explore a landscape of this character has many advantages. A zone of preservation uninterrupted by motorways, housing developments and other intrusions offers the possibility of observing an archaeological continuum, a surface in which the relationship between field and farmstead, trackway and burial ground may still be referenced. Another asset is the potential for a precise correlation to operate across the range of archaeological exploration techniques – aerial photography and ground survey keyed to the processes of archaeological excavation. The Porton landscape has permitted – indeed has encouraged – exploitation of these resources. It is a matter of good fortune that the site has now produced an author willing and able to demonstrate the fundamental importance of the Porton heritage in the archaeology of southern Britain.

Roy Canham
Wiltshire County Archaeologist, 2005

I

What is there and why it's there: by way of introduction

THE BREATH OF THE DRAGON

On 22 April 1915 the German Army, in an attempt to break the stalemate of trench warfare on the Western Front, released some 150 tons of chlorine gas from 5,500 cylinders against Allied forces, specifically the French 45th Division and their 87th Territorial Division, on a four-mile front of the Ypres Salient. Two days later, the Canadian forces in the Saint-Julien sector were similarly attacked. The British, in the form of the first battalion of the Dorset Regiment, were first attacked on 1 May. Clouds of choking gas enveloped the battlefield, inflicting many casualties, instilling fear and panic, but causing surprisingly few (but tragically painful) deaths in relation to the number of those incapacitated. The initial attack enabled the Germans to break through Allied lines, but their advantage was not followed through and was reversed by counter-attack, mainly because they were not convinced of the effectiveness of the new weapon beforehand.

Despite the French having deployed irritant gas shells – with little effect – against German strong points earlier in the war, the scale and initial effectiveness of the Ypres attacks resulted in 22 April 1915 being designated the birthdate of chemical warfare. It was then, too, that British generals decided they must also develop a 'capability in kind'. They also needed to master the chemical art of driving the enemy into cumbersome protective clothing and gas masks (1), degrading his ability to deploy and attack and to defend his ground, and burdening him with large numbers of casualties. The generals had their way; the British mounted their own gas attack using the same methods, and with a similar weight of chlorine, on 25 September, having taken six months to manufacture, transport and emplace the cylinders.

Long stretches of opposing front-line trenches on the Western Front were separated by a few scores of metres. The Germans and the British had simply to transport the

1 The British 'box respirator' of 1916. *Courtesy Defence CBRN Centre*

2 Canadian troops with respirators at Porton Down, 1918. *Courtesy DSTL*

thousands of commercial cylinders of gas to their front-lines, await a favourable wind, and open the valves at an appointed time. But the flaw lay in the weasel words 'await a favourable wind'. Rarely does the ebb and flow of war enable the luxury of waiting on a chance event; this is a necessary tactic suited to ships of war under sail. Also, when both sides released poison gas in this way, capricious winds wafted the clouds in unexpected directions, affecting friendly forces. Transportation and emplacement of gas in cylinders also presented a huge logistical problem. Necessity for surprise and the safety of one's friends demanded on-target delivery from a distance – artillery. Salvoes of shells, mortar bombs and canister projectiles were needed, abruptly placed on and upwind of the enemy who, mindful of the possibilities, sat waiting in his unwieldy protective gear, sweating, disorientated and restricted in his movements, his ability to fight severely degraded (2). Logistical problems were reduced greatly by employing shells charged with a highly volatile toxic liquid instead of large numbers of cylinders of compressed gas. This method also provided flexibility in attack, was suited to mobile warfare, and was less dependent on wind directions.

THE THICK END OF THE WEDGE

Military reasoning required that chemical munitions be developed and tested in the open air at some remote spot. Everyone knew that the prevailing wind in southern Britain came from the south-west, and that gas clouds expanded as they travelled downwind. A fan-shaped tract of land was essential, with its axis lying south-west to north-east, and long enough to permit poison clouds to dilute and disperse harmlessly before they crossed the north-east boundary. The terrain needed to be fairly flat and open, and remote from populated areas. Its requisitioning also had to impinge as little as possible on wartime agricultural production. A hill was necessary at the south-western end so that, in experiments employing artillery, gunners could see their targets clearly and simulate high angles of attack without resorting to inconvenient trajectories.

There were logistical requirements, too. The War Department Experimental Ground had ideally to be located near to Salisbury Plain, home to the many Army units. London-based generals and politicians needed swift and easy access to the site too. There was some compromise on these requirements, but surely few of the alternatives considered could have matched the suitability of what became known as Porton Down, or to the locals as 'the Camp'. The ground mostly consisted of gently undulating chalk downland: useful for grazing sheep but little else. At its south-western end rose the Iron Age hill-fort, Figsbury Ring (*colour plate 1*), on a prominence convenient for use as a firing point. Forming its north-western boundary ran the main line railway from London to Exeter, parallel to the Portway, the Roman road linking Old Sarum, north of Salisbury, with the Roman town of Calleva Atrebatum – Silchester. Brass hats and bowlers could alight at Porton railway station to arrive in time for lunch, having departed from Waterloo after a late breakfast. More importantly, by rail would come the thousands of tons of material needed to construct the Experimental Ground and keep it furnished with all its supplies.

Thus it was that the size, shape and location of the War Department Experimental Ground, Porton, came to be a gunners' blueprint, straddling the invisible line where Wiltshire met Hampshire, although not all of the land was acquired at once (*3*). As if to emphasise this 'between worlds' aspect of the Porton Range, it is now made up from the outermost elements of nine parishes: Winterbourne, Idmiston, Nether Wallop, Over Wallop, Winterslow, Newton Toney, Allington, Grateley and Firsdown (the latter parish being a subsequent creation). It is like the no-man's child of the fairy tale, its liminal qualities enhanced by its exclusive nature, an enchanted, secret, wild island amid an agro-desert. Currently, 2,800 hectares are in Ministry of Defence ownership, some 9km long and 4km at its widest, a permanent cartographic simulacrum of the deadly plumes of the past.

The generals and the mandarins had acquired an uninhabited and lowly developed landscape, with which they could do whatever the requirements of war dictated. Apart from the hill-fort with its grand and obvious architecture, and some barrows – boring-looking mounds of which there were thousands in the neighbourhood

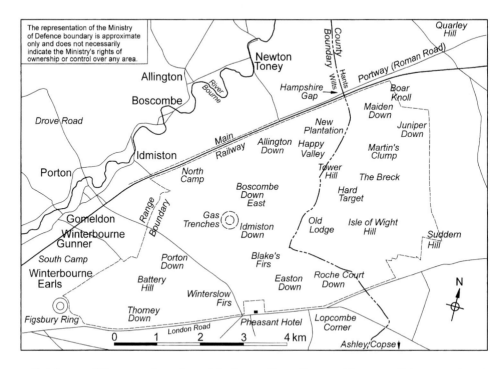

3 Sketch map of the present boundary of the Porton Down Range with names of places mentioned in the text. For more information, reference should be made to the Ordnance Survey Explorer 1:25,000 maps, sheets 130 and 131

– Whitehall's awareness and concern for the archaeology of the place was scant, if any. However, enclosure of the site in 1916 was a kindness to both the upstanding monuments and the buried antiquities, and soldiers seemed to respect them. Some of the land had never been ploughed, and much of the remainder only lightly so. Unlike the parlous existence of archaeological remains on the nearby Salisbury Plain Training Area (as now it is known), their counterparts at Porton were not at risk from mighty tracked vehicles uncertain of their way and anxious to dig in, nor from thousands of enthusiastically wielded entrenching tools. Damage inflicted by shells impacting on Porton Down was, by comparison, relatively light and confined to a few target areas. In contrast to the wholesale destruction wrought by the plough outside the Range boundary, the preservation of the past on the Range may justly be described as benevolent (*colour plate 2*).

And what a wealth of archaeology! Here are two major groups of Neolithic flint mines, six millennia old; over 100 round barrows of the Bronze Age; Bronze Age settlements, cemeteries and enclosures; Celtic fields overlaid by Iron Age linear features; a Saxon cemetery; an early ruined Georgian folly with its garden shrubs still flowering; a Napoleonic farm; the footings of a Victorian mansion with its pets' cemetery and ice house; sheep ponds; and the unique First World War experimental gas trenches, which are now a Scheduled Monument. Undoubtedly, much more awaits discovery.

It is unreasonable to suppose that the boundaries of this cornucopia of archaeology just happened to coincide with the gunners' blueprint, positioned as it was by the bureaucrats' coordinates, and that the chance consequences of war enclosed for posterity all the choicest morsels of prehistory lying between Salisbury and Stockbridge. Quite apart from the academic value of individual monuments and sites 'within the fence' and their corporate role in presenting one of the finest archaeological landscapes in Britain, is the telling message they convey that these cherished remnants of the past were once richly disposed across a much wider area and have been destroyed (and are being destroyed) through the activities of agriculture and development. With every additional loss outside its fence, the value of the monuments at Porton Down increases.

STEP BY STEP

From the beginning, there were two 'Camps'. North Camp was located at Porton Down and consisted of the Headquarters area – which housed the laboratories, workshops, administration and living accommodation – and the Range (or Ranges), on which outdoor investigations were conducted. The Trench Mortar Range (later the Army Chemical Warfare School) at Winterbourne Gunner was known as South Camp, and was destined to become a separate establishment.

The military and scientific history of both 'Camps' has been admirably chronicled by Gradon Carter in his *Chemical and biological defence at Porton Down, 1916–2000*, although none of the histories of Porton Down mentions that it was first associated with military activity in 1898. Under the Military Manoeuvres Act of 1887 50,000 troops were assembled at Porton Down before they marched to the reviewing area at Boscombe Down West. The exercise was reported in the *Salisbury and Winchester Journal* of 10 September 1898 under the headline of 'A Splendid Spectacle'; and vast crowds assembled to watch it. A detailed account of the acquisition of the Porton Down lands is provided by Keith Norris in his *History of the Porton lands* and *Development of the Porton campus*. In this present volume we shall explore the microcosm of archaeology that is the Porton Down Range, examining the sites, monuments and artefacts, and setting them within their contemporary contexts in a more generously expansive landscape, working our way through time. First, though, let us examine the basic features of the terrain, for these are the major determinants of human activity, the nature of mankind's monuments, and the survival of his detritus. Then, briefly at this point, we shall relate Porton Down's landscape to the familiar, if not entirely adequate, fashionable archaeological chronology of stone, bronze and iron.

Porton Down lies wholly on what is termed the Upper Chalk, although we shall need to refine this classification later. Within the chalk occur nodules of flint, a microcrystalline rock composed almost entirely of silica. We speak casually of 'the Stone Age', thus implying that stone (more correctly, stone implements) was the dominant feature of that culture; in fact, it was only the most durable. 'Stone' for the chalk lands means flint; its abundance and suitability for fashioning implements resulted in flint mining and knapping industries becoming established on the downs. The first flint knappers belonged to the Lower Palaeolithic period, when humans shared the landscape with woolly mammoths. It is certain that man lived on the chalk downland around Porton at this time. The last ice age reached down to Berkshire, and when the ice sheet melted, some 12,000 years ago, it sent torrents of water raging through our landscape, sculpting many of the valleys and defining the hills and plateaux. The water swept away most of the sands and gravels where they overlaid the high chalk, depositing them in lower areas, such as the Milford Hill gravels near Salisbury. Axes and other implements of the Palaeolithic period, more ancient than the ice, have been recovered from these deposits (*4*).

Flint working was most prolific and most artful in the Neolithic period at Porton (say from 4000–2000 BC). Evidence of Mesolithic peoples (10,000–4000 BC) is tenuous at Porton Down, although there are numerous Mesolithic sites dotted along the high chalk ridge spanning the southern counties, and it is reasonable to suppose with more certainty that Mesolithic man dwelt at Porton, too, and has left behind his belongings and his rubbish. Some items of worked flint found at Porton Down have been identified as of Mesolithic origin. Flint as a raw material for the manufacture of implements remained important well into the Bronze Age (2000–700 BC), for

4 Lower
Palaeolithic hand
axe from the
gravel deposits

bronze tools and weapons were far too costly to employ universally (5). By this time
there are firm signs of settlement patterns at Porton Down, with a major farmstead
on Thorney Down Hill, Celtic field boundaries, and cremation burial cemeteries
that appear to respect and reinforce tribal boundaries.

Chalk downland bears mainly thin soils. These humic layers are supportive of grass
and shrub species, which produce seeds and fruit, and so form habitats for insects, and
hence birds, small mammals, roe deer and red deer. Once there were wild pigs and
wolves here too. Patchy woodland covered much of the area. Hunter–gatherers could,
and obviously did, successfully exploit such environments, if only at low population
densities. But from the Neolithic period onwards communities included farmers,
growing crops and herding or corralling animals. With an increased and secure supply
of food, populations could expand, and did so. Such was the pattern of life over
the great swath of chalk stretching from Dorset, through Hampshire, Wiltshire and
Berkshire then branching up through Buckinghamshire, Suffolk and Norfolk, and
down to Sussex and Kent. But obtaining water must have been a problem for all
downland dwellers, as it is today for many deprived tropical communities. It has always
been assumed that Porton Down's population solved the problem in the same manner
as thirsty African people of today do, by carrying it long distances, in this case from
the River Bourne. (An eminent archaeologist at Porton, whom we shall meet later,
when queried about the problem, revealed the cultural bias present in archaeological
interpretation of the time by replying: 'No doubt they sent their womenfolk down to
the river.' He also considered a skeleton found with a necklace to be that of a woman,
for the reason of adornment.) Later Porton communities dug dew-ponds for their
sheep and sank wells for themselves. The water problem was solved in one way or
another, and its existence must not be construed as rendering downland as marginally
habitable territory, although proximity to water no doubt added value to some areas.

5 Bronze axe from the Bronze Age discovered by chance at Porton Down

As we shall discuss in greater detail later, it is the Upper Chalk plateaux and hilltops that contain the best and most easily obtainable flint nodules, those suitable for fashioning into tools and weapons. Almost by definition, these are the regions most remote from water sources, but they were successfully and probably cheerfully colonised.

By the Iron Age (700 BC–AD 80), chalk and flint in themselves ceased to figure large in the economy and culture of the population, but the topography of the chalk downland, with extensive plateaux, sharp valley scarps and prominent hills, is eminently suited to defining and protecting tribal territories. Figsbury Ring, as we have noted, is an Iron Age feature and, although its primary use is uncertain (defensive, protective or ritual), it bespeaks a vigorous Iron Age community. The great tribal centre of Danebury Hill, less than 5km to the east of the Range boundary, and its garrison outlier, Quarley Hill, just to the north of the boundary, make it clear that the now circumscribed tract of Porton Down was an integral part of a much larger, organised fiefdom (6). A lengthy stretch of a bank and ditch feature runs southwards from Thruxton Hill, through Quarley hill-fort and across the Range to Ashley Copse, just beyond the Range's boundary. As a major endeavour of civil engineering its function appears more than a mere boundary marker, although it does not approach in size the massive defensive earthwork of Bokerley Dyke, 15km south-west of Salisbury. An exploratory trench placed across this 'Quarley High Linear' on Porton Down in 1984 revealed the multi-layered, palimpsest nature of the site, for the Iron Age feature's bank had sealed a Bronze Age land surface, and its ditch was revetted with waste material from nearby Neolithic flint mines; this revetment had been quarried by later gunflint knappers, and the bank thus flattened was used in the nineteenth or early twentieth century as a farm cart track. For good measure, Saxon burials were found in this Iron Age ditch near Roche Court Down.

The Roman period is only sparsely represented at Porton Down: the existence of the Portway meant that the Romans literally passed it by. There have been isolated sherds of Roman pottery discovered, but nothing indicative of a settlement. Lack of water *was* a problem for the Romans, who used more of it than previous inhabitants, especially for their social ablutions. Their solution was to settle in places with abundant water. All the known Roman towns and villas lie near watercourses.

Water supply was not a problem for the Saxons, Idma and Porta, for example, who gave their names to Idmiston and Porton; they forsook the high ground and colonised the river valleys. From this time onwards the downland became mainly the preserve of sheep whose wool provided the wealth by which medieval Salisbury was built and maintained, and on which the country's economy relied. Sheep were also the engine by which nutrients from the downs were transferred to the folded areas of arable in the valleys and this action served to ensure an abundance of grain could be grown. Apart from the Victorian estate and its farm, and a little subsistence farming elsewhere, shepherding remained the main occupation on the downs up to the creation of the Porton Down Range.

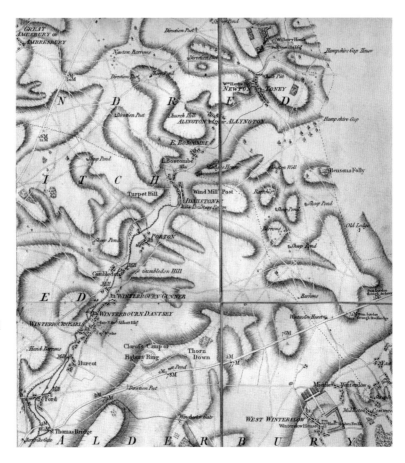

6 A section of the Andrews and Dury map of Wiltshire, 1773, showing areas now part of the Porton Down Range. *Courtesy Bourne Valley Historical Society*

The perception of what constitutes archaeology changes with time. The remains from both World Wars are now being catalogued and scheduled as archaeological monuments. One of Porton Down's major archaeological features is the now scarcely discernible ring of gas trenches dug in 1916, judged by archaeologists as worthy of protection. But there are others that have served their purpose and stand on ground needed for current operational reasons. They need to be recorded before they disappear, for they will become archaeology one day.

AMATEURS TO THE RESCUE

At this point, while the discussion remains of a general nature, the reader's attention is drawn to the valuable and enjoyable volume by Martin Green: *A landscape revealed: 10,000 years on a chalkland farm*. The farm is Down Farm in north Dorset, owned by Green, and lying within Cranborne Chase, athwart the Dorset Cursus, a 9.6km-long pair of parallel earthen banks constructed in the Neolithic period. Long barrows mark its northern and southern terminals, and the surrounding area is strewn with a multitude of later Bronze Age round barrows. This is clearly a ritual landscape, and Green has discovered and excavated other structures, some also of a ritual nature. Down Farm and the Porton Down Range, both conveniently bounded areas of chalk downland with evidence of intense activity in similar prehistoric times, cannot be directly compared. Particularly in the Neolithic period and the Bronze Age, though, they allow different partial views of societies with characteristic domestic and religious components.

Cranborne Chase was the purlieu of General Pitt Rivers, who necessarily changed his name from Lane Fox on inheriting the Rushmore estate. Pitt Rivers is often described as the father of British archaeology because of his insistence on thorough stratigraphical excavation, meticulous record keeping, and full publication of the results, all of which he funded himself. With Pitt Rivers we observe the evolution of the antiquarian into the archaeologist.

Particularly in the nineteenth and early twentieth centuries, amateur archaeologists, operating either alone or through county archaeological societies, performed most work on British archaeology. It was a respectable occupation for educated gentlemen, especially the clergy and those of means. In 1925, in this tradition of general scholarship, but needing to earn his living, Dr J.F.S. Stone stepped into the Porton Down landscape. A chemist by profession, he seemed less interested in rearranging the molecular bonds among the elements than in indulging his passion for archaeology. He it was who discovered the richness of the prehistoric landscape, dug it up, and published a stream of reports on it. In so doing he put Porton Down on the archaeological map. Much of what we know about the place is due to his untiring efforts, and he will be constantly referenced in this story. We had best now make his acquaintance.

2

J.F.S. Stone:
the man and his works

John Frederick Smerdon Stone was born in Bath in 1899 and educated at Monkton Coombe School near that city from 1909 to 1913. He became a prefect, an oarsman and captain of rugby football. In 1917, he spent one term as a schoolmaster at Monkton Coombe before joining the Royal Garrison Artillery (RGA) as a first lieutenant in 1918. The RGA was responsible for coastal defence, and it manned mountain batteries. Leaving the Army in 1920, after a further term as schoolmaster at Monkton Coombe, he went up to Wadham College, Oxford, to read chemistry, and after graduating in 1923, stayed on to do research there. He demonstrated his academic versatility by producing two scientific papers on completely different topics, one on photosynthesis, the other on the action of halides on dimethylbenzoyl chloride. He was awarded his PhD in 1925 and took a job at what was then the Chemical Warfare Experimental Station, buying a house at Ford, near Winterbourne Earls, 2km east of Old Sarum.

To his friends, Stone was always known as 'Marcus', after Marcus Stone, a well-known painter and illustrator of books by Dickens and Trollope, who died in 1921. Perhaps Stone's own artistic abilities won him this nickname. In 1927 he married Emily Brown, an American with dual nationality. They had no children. The photograph of Stone shows him at Stonehenge in 1954 (7); compare this picture with his bookplate (19).

Within two years, with the enthusiasm of a newcomer, Stone produced four research reports on the production of aerosols using pyrotechnics, a technique still employed to disseminate insecticides in greenhouses. But then his research reports dried up: he had discovered the archaeology of the 'Porton Experimental Ground'. Perhaps he had read the report of the excavation of the nearby Figsbury Ring by Maud Cunnington, which appeared in 1928, as by 1930 he began to keep a manuscript notebook, 'Notes on Excavations' that eventually ran to two volumes;

7 Marcus Stone at Stonehenge in 1954. *Courtesy Bourne Valley Historical Society*

these are housed in the library of the Salisbury and South Wiltshire Museum. (Volume II was discovered in private possession in 1989, and the Museum's copy is a facsimile.) While this chapter covers the main points of Stone's archaeological career, the more important discoveries relating to Porton Down, much of which was reported in *The Wiltshire Archaeological and Natural History Magazine*, will be dealt with in greater detail later.

Stone's first excavation was of a Bronze Age barrow lying in a field near the Pheasant Hotel on the London Road, where he had lodged on joining the staff of the Chemical Warfare Experimental Ground. He performed this work with A.T.Wicks, a noted authority on Somerset's barrows, who had succeeded Stone as a schoolmaster at Monkton Coombe in 1921. Mindful of the wholesale damage wreaked by early barrow diggers, Stone wrote in his notebook that 'Unnecessary explorations in barrows are rightly to be deprecated'. But he justified his own excavation as a limitation of damage, for rabbits had removed the greater part of a skeleton, which had lain under a cairn of flints and had been inserted in the barrow on top of a bucket-shaped urn of the Late Bronze Age. There were no other grave goods, and the skeleton was presumed to be of Early Iron Age or Romano-British origin.

In 1929, Stone was mapping the trackways, ditches and barrows south of the River Bourne with the aid of that most useful of new tools, aerial photography. It became obvious to him that the linear features converged on Easton Down. A closer examination of the area revealed some 90 artificial depressions in the ground over an area of about 16 hectares, strewn with knapped flint flakes and broken tools.

He excavated the area between 1930 and 1934, discovering a group of Neolithic flint mines (*colour plate 3*) and a Beaker period settlement. (The Beaker period, approximately 2500–1700 BC, spanned the late Neolithic period and Early Bronze Age, being characterised by a cultural package that included characteristically shaped ceramic vessels named Beakers.)

Stone displayed scant regard for his safety during these excavations. Photographs show that he used a makeshift Jacob's ladder for access to his pits. He discusses, too, the absence of galleries to the mines:

> … the chalk though well bedded is not very secure and falls from the undercut roof must
> have occurred thus prohibiting the driving of galleries. This was brought home forcibly to
> the author whilst clearing the undercuttings. Twice a fall occurred, about two tons coming
> away from the east side and about one ton from the west.

The Easton Down work was interrupted in 1930, when a rabbit trapper informed Stone that human bones had been found near Lopcombe Corner on Roche Court Down. On excavation, he discovered 18 male skeletons, nine of which had been decapitated. Four had their hands tied behind their backs (*8*). His interpretation was that these were Saxon or Jute invaders killed by the Romano-British inhabitants in the fifth or sixth centuries. They had been buried in an Iron Age ditch, the Quarley High Linear. In 1935, he and Sir Norman Gray Hill excavated a similar cemetery on Stockbridge Down, further south in Hampshire, where 26 skeletons were discovered, mostly male; further disturbed bones suggested there had been 36 bodies in all. They had been buried at different times. Some had their wrists bound. Two of them had been decapitated with the skulls placed between their legs. Six silver coins of Edward the Confessor, originally wrapped in cloth, were found under the left armpit of one such body; the bones of a large dog, minus its skull, lay between the thighs (*9*). Stone suggested that these burials were those of robbers or transgressors of the harsh game laws of the time.

Stone discovered three small barrows sited close to the Roche Court Down burials, one of which contained a Saxon inhumation of a man 6ft (1.8m) tall, buried with a sixth-century iron knife and the remains of a leg of mutton. Forty yards north of these lay a Christian cemetery with 13 graves. Two iron knives were found there, together with another leg of mutton. Analysis of the skeletons, their dispositions in their graves and the provision of grave goods, suggested to Stone that this was a normal Saxon cemetery to which he tentatively ascribed a date of the sixth or seventh century.

Also in 1933, Stone discovered a cemetery of the Bronze Age overlying, or perhaps on the edge of, the Neolithic flint mine site on Easton Down. He had already unearthed a settlement of the same period there and was delighted to find a ritual monument exhibiting probable associations with the mines. This 'urnfield', as he

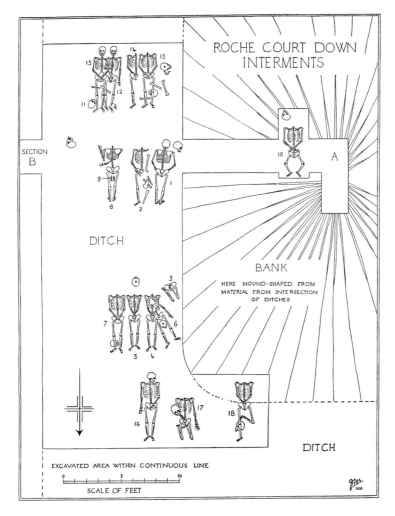

ROCHE COURT DOWN
INTERMENTS

SECTION
B

A

DITCH

BANK

HERE MOUND-SHAPED FROM
MATERIAL FROM INTERSECTION
OF DITCHES

DITCH

EXCAVATED AREA WITHIN CONTINUOUS LINE

0   5   10

SCALE OF FEET

8 Roche Court Down Saxon burials discovered by Marcus Stone. Courtesy WANHM

called the cemetery, consisted of a low (15cm) platform 18 x 6m in size composed of large flints, including waste material and damaged tools from the flint mining and knapping industry. Under the flints he discovered several small pits, or 'cists', four of them with funerary urns, one of which contained a bead made from faience, a form of glassware that originated in ancient Egypt. Yet another ritual monument was discovered bordering the flint mines, a small barrow containing a skull against which stood a large bar of roughly chipped flint, optimistically described in the text by Stone as suggestive of a phallus but downgraded to an 'implement' in the caption to his illustration, and later referred to as 'a bar' (*colour plate 4*). Such burials of severed heads are known as 'cephalotaphic' by archaeologists.

These were certainly busy days, for in 1933 Stone was also engaged, with J. Charlton, in a trial excavation in the eastern suburb of Old Sarum, Salisbury. This was the site of the former town of Salisbury with its first cathedral and castle set within

9 Decapitated skeleton from Stockbridge Down with the bones of a headless dog. *Courtesy H.M. Darlow*

the confines of an Iron Age hill-fort. In 1075 it was decided to move the cathedral and town to its present location following arguments between the monks of the cathedral and the castle's garrison. John Leland wrote in his *Itinerary* in 1540 that there were two gates to Old Sarum, east and west, with a suburb outside each, in the east of which there stood a parish church dedicated to St John the Baptist. The construction of the new main road past the Castle Inn in 1931 had revealed only a few fragments of pottery, but the digging of a cesspit by a farmer near Old Sarum disclosed four skeletons which, he claimed, had iron nails through their hands. The excavation revealed the foundation of a building with graves surrounding it. Fragments of stone and marble from the thirteenth century were found, and it was thought that this was the church of St John destroyed in 1548. Four Norman cesspits were dug out, and at the bottom of one lay a silver coin of William the Conqueror. Stone remembered that dig, for he received a bucket of ancient night-soil on his head while absorbed with the silver coin!

The discovery of the Easton Down flint mines had been a major event and raised Stone's status from a chemist who practised archaeology as a hobby, to that of a competent archaeologist. His reputation was enhanced further when the International Congress of Prehistory and Protohistory Societies visited Easton Down to view the site, in the August of 1932. Then, in 1933, he discovered another group of 100 or so flint mines at Martin's Clump, only 3.6km from the Easton Down group. The discerning reader can observe, from the spate of excavations and publications at this period, that

Stone was probably overstretched on the archaeological front. It is no wonder, then, that the examination of the Martin's Clump flint mines was put on hold, except for the excavation of one of the 'workshop floors', areas of industrial flint knapping. The Second World War crept up on him and he was called to exercise his energies and talents at Porton Down in the service of his country. He did still have time for some archaeological work, as we shall see, but he did not excavate a mine shaft at Martin's Clump. Instead, he asked the senior military officer at Porton, Lt Col James Watson, and his wife Barbara, to examine one in 1954. Owing to the untimely and sudden death of Marcus Stone in 1957, the Watsons' excavation report was unfortunately lost; however, with the help of Mrs Watson, a retrospective report on this excavation was compiled and published over 40 years later by the author. A further glimpse of the Martin's Clump complex was obtained in 1984 when four mines, lying outside the known area, were damaged by a mechanical digger during trenching operations to lay a cable.

However, the Porton Down Range and its antiquities did not demand all the energies of this fit and active man in his mid-thirties. Stone's friend and aide in his excavations, Commander H.G. Higgins, owned a house named 'The Croft' on the Portway lying between Old Sarum and Winterbourne Earls. In 1932, while constructing an orchard, Higgins noticed dark patches in the freshly cut faces of the chalk. On excavation, Stone discovered these to be silted up dwelling pits of late Neolithic date, containing a flint axe and sherds of Peterborough ware (a characteristic round-bottomed bowl, decorated with bone and cord impressions). Close to these pits lay a severely damaged Iron Age ditch that ran towards the River Bourne with post-holes either side. Stone interpreted the ditch as a cattle drove between cultivated fields, a view that was to impact on opinions regarding linear bank and ditch 'systems' for many years, indeed, until the present. Then, in 1934, Stone helped his old friend A.T. Wicks excavate an enclosure at Hayes Wood in Somerset. The site lies within a mile of Monkton Coombe. Stone was digging on home territory.

The presence of a number of Royal Air Force airfields, including Old Sarum, near Salisbury, provided the opportunity for aerial photography, for which Stone was a great enthusiast. Aircraft from Old Sarum used the landing strip close to Stone's laboratory, and this may have allowed him to obtain the aerial photographs he used so successfully. Crop marks and soil marks were new and exciting tools in the 1920s. A photograph of a barrow known as Ende Burgh, to the north-east of Old Sarum, depicted many archaeological features (*10*). He commissioned further photographs of the same site that revealed a group of 12 ploughed-out and unrecorded barrows and two ploughed-out enclosures with their associated ditches. One of the enclosures was of rectangular appearance, of Roman date. Trench digging in the area in 1935 revealed two small cists containing cremations, one of them associated with a miniature urn 10cm tall, dating to the Late Bronze Age.

Stone made a major discovery in 1936 during a planned survey of the southern downland scarps between Figsbury Ring and Roche Court Down. His aerial

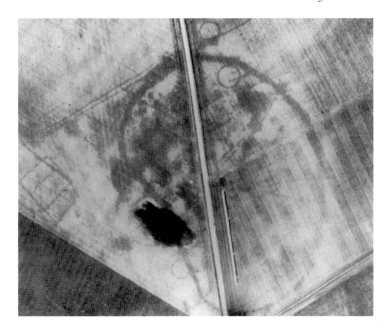

10 Marcus Stone's aerial photograph of Ende Burgh. *Courtesy H.M. Darlow*

photographs displayed a chequerboard of ancient cultivation beneath the modern ploughsoil. On Thorney Down he discovered an isolated ditch, but his efforts to map the disturbed terrain coherently – even with the aid of further photography – proved unsuccessful. The existence of lynchets and newly discovered barrows on this patch of uncultivated downland, and the numerous pottery sherds thrown up by rabbits, enticed him to excavate. He found a series of post-holes, interpreting them as representing nine small dwellings, a family smallholding. Domestic artefacts and a double-looped bronze spearhead were also recovered. However, interpretation of the mass of post-holes was far from straightforward; Ann Ellison wrote of the site: 'The settlement plan has provided one of the classic post-hole games employed in modern archaeological teaching.' Even Professor Stuart Piggott had a go, not too successfully. Ellison provided a modern interpretation using comparable analogues from elsewhere in addition to the pattern of the holes, which will be discussed in Chapter 5.

Stone was asked to investigate a ditch found at Ratfyn, 1.6km from Woodhenge, a prehistoric ritual circle composed of wooden posts lying 2.5km north-east of Stonehenge that had been discovered by aerial photography in 1925, excavated by Maud Cunnington between 1926 and 1929. Here he discovered 'Halberd-shaped' arrowheads, a hammer, axe and pottery sherds that enabled him to date the ditch to the Early Bronze Age and relate them to the 'Woodhenge Culture'.

Stone's next excavation was truly a research project, in that it was conducted to answer a specific question. He discovered a rectangular enclosure on Boscombe Down East, on the Porton Down Range, consisting of three sides of a bank and ditch abutting a lengthy linear earthwork. The logical sequence appeared to be that the enclosure

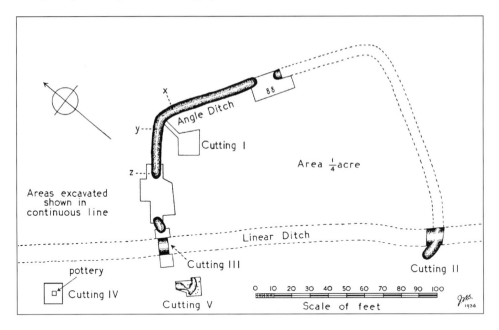

11 Marcus Stone's drawing of the Bronze Age enclosure on Boscombe Down East. *Courtesy WANHM*

builders had economised on their building efforts by utilising the extant third side (*11*, *12*). Stone threw doubt on this assumption by carefully excavating the abutment points: the enclosure was of Bronze Age date while the linear feature appeared to be of later Iron Age construction. He also discovered nearby what he interpreted as 'a dwelling pit of the Beaker Culture', with a causeway containing evidence of gateposts leading to the enclosure. The infill of the ditch contained potsherds, flint flakes, scrapers, cores, hammerstones, pot-boilers (nodular flints or large pebbles placed in the fire and plunged into pots of water to heat them up), bone awls and a profusion of animal bones, some from a small horse, proving that particular animal's presence in this country in the Bronze Age. There was also a stone axe of Cornish origin. Like the faience bead from his urnfield on Easton Down, this latter find was to lead to a large part of his later work on archaeology. In recent years, Martin Green was to discover a Middle Bronze Age enclosure of similar shape at Down Farm, enclosing a longhouse; however, the Down Farm enclosure was 10 times the length of Stone's.

The Winterslow Hut group of round barrows had been known for many years. In 1814, the Rev Allan Borman Hutchins, whose father had an estate at Porton, excavated one of them, and later another. At that date barrows were invariably dug without any record being made of their structure or contents but, remarkably, the contents were painted in oils on canvas by a Thomas Guest of Salisbury. Although the existence of these paintings was known, they had been lost, but with the help of Mr Frank Stevens, the Curator of Salisbury Museum, Stone made extensive and persistent enquiries to locate them. They now reside in the Salisbury and South

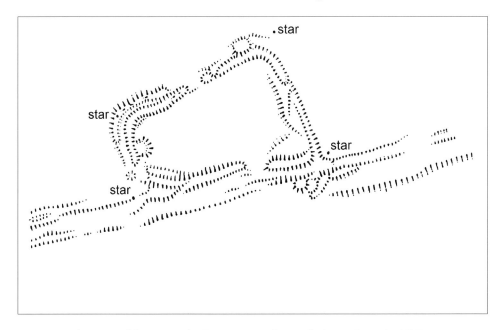

12 RCHME's survey of the Boscombe Down East enclosure. © *Crown Copyright. NMR*

Wiltshire Museum, and the artefacts from the barrow are in the custody of the Ashmolean Museum at Oxford. The excavations by Hutchins are described more fully in Chapter 5. With the aid of aerial photographs, Stevens and Stone were able to identify a further six barrows in the cemetery, bringing to 21 the total of known barrows in the Winterslow Hut group (*13*).

Roughly 1km north of Stonehenge, and disposed approximately east–west, lies the Stonehenge Cursus, parallel banks about 100m apart and 2.8km long, discovered by the antiquarian William Stukeley in 1723. Until recently, its western terminal was partly in Fargo Wood. In 1937, Stone's attention was drawn to a number of potsherds, picked up from a rabbit burrow in the wood by two Boy Scouts. They came from a food-vessel rarely found in Wessex but common in the north of England, and the possibility that a site near Stonehenge would provide evidence of cultural links with the north of the country seemed very exciting. On excavation, a grave was discovered, partly surrounded by an asymmetrical ditch 1.5m wide and 1.4m deep (*14*), within which lay a carefully excavated multiple grave with four burials. Three of these were inhumations and the fourth was a cremation burial. A crushed Beaker, 15cm tall, of a pattern originating in the north-east of the country (*15*), lay in the grave together with a food-vessel 13cm tall (*16*). Rabbit disturbance and the later insertion of cremated remains prevented Stone from establishing whether the four burials had been contemporaneous (he suspected that one was a secondary interment), but the presence together of the Beaker and the food-vessel prompted him to speculate that the burial was from the earliest introduction of the practice of cremation burial to Wessex.

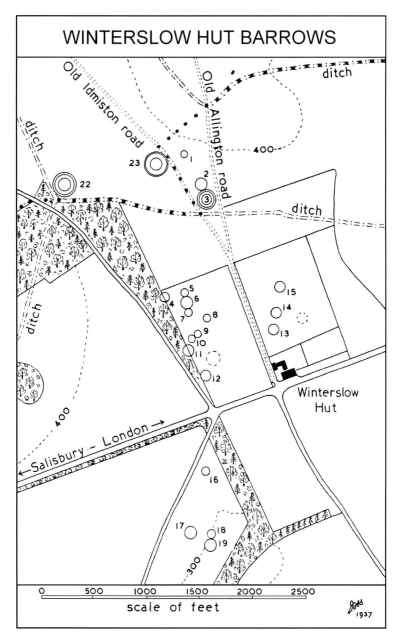

13 The Winterslow Hut (Pheasant Hotel) group of round barrows. *Courtesy WANHM*

1 Figsbury Ring with its outer bank and ditch and inner ditch. The firing positions for the guns are on the left of the hill-fort

2 The north-eastern boundary of the downland showing the contrast with the agricultural area

3 Remains of the Neolithic flint mines on Easton Down

4 The cephalotaphic skull and flint 'bar' from a barrow on Easton Down. *Courtesy Salisbury Museum*

5 Beads and bone awl from Stone's 'urnfield' on Easton Down. The faience bead is top left. *Courtesy Salisbury Museum*

6 Beads and bronze awl from Blake's Firs cremation cemetery

7 Miniature Collared Urn (Urn 1) from Blake's Firs cremation cemetery

8 Cremation pit at Blake's Firs showing evidence of penetration by a rabbit burrow

9 Oil painting by Thomas Guest showing the contents of a cremation burial in Hutchins' 'bell barrow of chalk'. *Courtesy Salisbury Museum*

10 Transitional Late Bronze Age/Early Iron Age urn, 39cm tall with 42cm diameter rim, discovered south of Idmiston Road at Porton Down. *Courtesy Salisbury Museum*

11 The Winterslow Great Barrow with Battery Hill and Thorney Down Wood on the horizon. *Courtesy John Jochimsen*

12 The D-feature enclosure and the round barrow on its apex

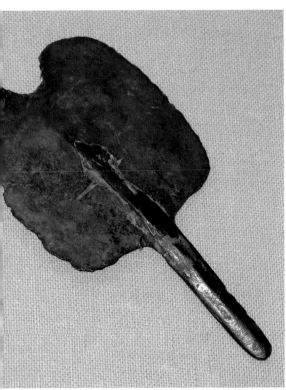

13 *Left* Bronze bifid razor of the Bronze Age, 10.1cm long, found in a rabbit scrape on Battery Hill. *Courtesy Salisbury Museum*

14 *Right* Ewart Park pattern bronze sword, 60cm long, found in 1704 during ploughing at Figsbury Ring. *Courtesy Salisbury Museum*

15 *Below* Danebury hill-fort. © *Copyright English Heritage. NMR*

16 Above Saxon necklace of glass and amber beads with bronze shoulder brooch, 6.1cm in diameter, from Winterbourne Gunner cemetery. *Courtesy Salisbury Museum*

17 Left Saxon iron artefacts from Winterbourne Gunner cemetery. *Courtesy Salisbury Museum*

18 Below Saxon bronze perforated spoon, 10cm in length, from Winterbourne Gunner cemetery. *Courtesy Salisbury Museum*

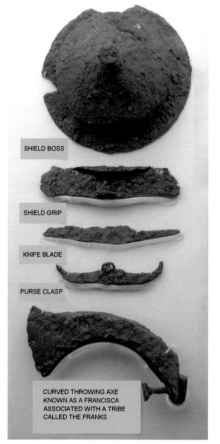

SHIELD BOSS

SHIELD GRIP

KNIFE BLADE

PURSE CLASP

CURVED THROWING AXE KNOWN AS A FRANCISCA ASSOCIATED WITH A TRIBE CALLED THE FRANKS

19 The mound of debris from Benson's Folly on Tower Hill

20 The 'valley of the stones' on Tower Hill with masonry blocks from Benson's Folly

21 A stone stair tread found on Tower Hill

22 A masonry block from Tower Hill which fits the stair tread

Opposite
23 An example of wild flower growth at Porton Down resulting from ground disturbance the previous year

24 Lichen-rich grassland in Isle of Wight woods

25 Mounds of the yellow meadow ant, covered in rockrose with old, dying juniper on Easton Down

26, 27, 28 and 29 Dogs' graves at Old Lodge

30, 31 and 32 Dogs' graves at Old Lodge

33 The grave of Wilbury the racehorse in Isle of Wight Wood, 1907

34 Tableware from the Old Lodge domestic rubbish dump made for Messrs Watson and Godden 1860-70 for the tourist trade, showing Salisbury's Cathedral and Poultry Cross. Watson's still thrives in Salisbury

35 The night soil-bucket from Old Lodge

36 The cast iron well head by Tasker & Sons, restored as a conservation project

37 An artist's impression of the Headquarters building begun in 1918

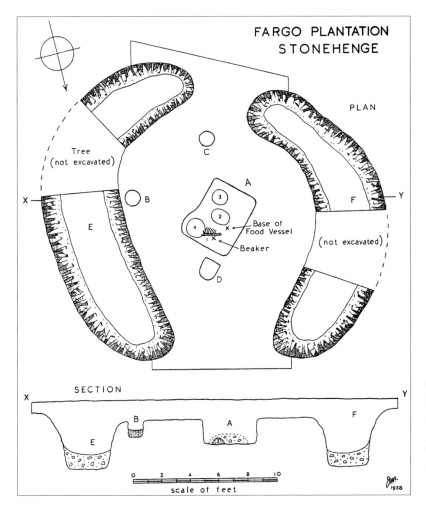

FARGO PLANTATION
STONEHENGE

PLAN

Tree
(not excavated)

C

A

X — B

E

3

2

1

Base of
Food Vessel

Beaker

D

F — Y

(not excavated)

SECTION

X

B

A

F

Y

E

0   2   4   6   8   10

scale of feet

1938

14 The
graves
in Fargo
Wood, near
Stonehenge,
discovered
by Marcus
Stone.
Courtesy
WANHM

    Close to the base of the ditch in Fargo Wood lay a fragment of rhyolite, one of the rocks from which the bluestones at Stonehenge are fashioned. Stone's commitment to the war effort prevented him from immediate investigation, but he returned to the scene in 1947 when he sectioned the Cursus itself, discovering another rhyolite fragment. A search of the nearby ploughed field revealed 10 more, causing him to speculate that there had once been a bluestone monument there, which induced him to believe that the Cursus was contemporary with both the Aubrey holes and the circular ditch of Stonehenge. (The holes, or pits, forming a ring within the earthen circle, are named after the antiquarian John Aubrey who surveyed Stonehenge at the command of Charles II.)

    The rich archaeology surrounding Stonehenge had long been a source of interest to antiquarians. Julian Richards records that over 300 barrows have been dug there, often at the rate of several a day. The famous Bush Barrow, excavated by William

15 Left: Beaker vessel from the Fargo Wood graves. *Courtesy H.M. Darlow*

16 Above: Food vessel from the Fargo Wood graves. *Courtesy H.M. Darlow*

Cunnington in 1808 and richly endowed with gold objects, was no doubt a spur to this activity. While twentieth-century archaeological investigation had concentrated on Stonehenge itself, Stone's work made an attempt to understand the landscape in which it stood, a movement that culminated in the Royal Commission on Historical Monuments of England's survey of Stonehenge and its Environs and subsequently English Heritage's Stonehenge Environs Project led by Richards.

Stone was promoted to the grade of Senior Scientific Officer in 1938, and he moved house from Ford to 'The Poplars' in Winterbourne Gunner, where both he and his wife became involved in the social life of the village. Stone was elected a Vice President of the Winterbourne Cricket Club. Despite the increased professional demands on him caused by war he, together with Colonel Sir Norman Gray Hill (who was killed in an aircraft accident in 1944), excavated a barrow on Stockbridge Down composed of flint nodules, amongst and around which were potsherds of the Beaker period, the Middle Bronze Age and the Romano-British period. The primary grave lay in the centre of the barrow which was surrounded by an unusual, shallow ditch with five well-marked causeways. The only other example of this kind was the burial excavated by Stone at Fargo Wood. The interment was accompanied by a large Beaker 20cm tall. Inserted into the barrow were three later cremation burials. One was in an inverted urn 40cm tall which held the burnt bones of a child about 15 years old, a large number of beads, and a bronze awl. The beads were of segmented faience, amber, calcite (the first to be recognised in Britain), jet, shale and lignite. This burial and its grave goods would relate very strongly to a cairn, or flint nodule barrow which was excavated on the Porton Down Range in 1983–95 and is described in Chapter 5.

New building work on a part of the Porton Down estate known as South Camp, which is now the separate establishment of the Defence Chemical, Biological, Radiological and Nuclear Centre, Winterbourne Gunner, began in 1939. A mechanical digger unearthed a crudely made, undecorated pygmy cup (*17*), a small funerary vessel which may have held food offerings or incense. Although aerial photographs had not revealed the presence of a barrow, Stone attributed this find to a Late Bronze Age cremation burial.

During the war years, Stone became the Technical Administrator of a special group formed to assess the threat from biological attacks by the enemy. His knowledge and enthusiasm were in great demand; his methodical approach to problems, so evident in his archaeological work, was highly valued by his colleagues. His natural diplomacy and courtesy, and his insistence on treating everyone as an equal, won him friends and allies. There is a break in the entries in his excavation notebook from April 1938 to October 1947, but then Stone began pursuing his archaeology again, encouraging his colleagues to interest themselves in archaeology, of whom at least half a dozen did. Among these was John Musty, a chemist with archaeological qualifications. Musty excavated with Stone and was encouraged by him to undertake independent excavations. Later, Musty became the head of the newly formed Ancient Monuments Laboratory and a Fellow of the Society of Antiquaries, an honour already bestowed on Stone, who was by now regarded as an authority on prehistory.

Shortly before the war, the museums and art galleries in the south-west of England formed a committee to study the petrological composition and origins of stone axes in their possession. Their first report was issued in 1941. By taking small sections of the material of the axe and grinding them down so that they could be examined under the microscope, it was possible to determine the quarry from which the stone had come. By drawing maps showing the distribution of finds of axes made from a particular rock, the movement of material along particular routes might be established. As mentioned above, it may have been Stone's find of a Cornish axe that made him

17 The pygmy cup from Winterbourne Dauntsey. *Courtesy Salisbury Museum*

take a great interest in the work of the committee, and by 1947 he had become joint secretary of it. He contributed a chapter to a book published in France by A. Laming on the use of axes to define trade routes. By his death in 1957, over 1,000 axes had been sliced, and over 400 placed in one of 24 groups; by 1988 that total had risen to 7,600.

In 1948, Stone excavated two pits, each covered by a cairn of flints, about 1.2m in diameter discovered in Countess Road, Amesbury, only 300m from Woodhenge. They were found to be full of ash, and contained 972 flint flakes, 8 flint saws, 13 flint scrapers, 7 petit tranchet arrowheads, 10 bone pins or awls, 1 hammerstone, 3 sarsen fragments, 7 pot-boilers, 2 antler picks, 4 marine shells, 2 stone axes (one of North Wales origin), 1 flint knife and 5 flint balls, animal bones and numerous sherds of Grooved ware pottery (Late Neolithic vessels often associated with ceremonial sites). Many of the implements were fresh, so the pits did not constitute rubbish dumps; Stone considered them to be ritualistic in nature.

Stone returned to Stockbridge Down the same year where he excavated a Beaker period inhumation in which was discovered a Beaker 16cm in height, which he describes as 'a very poor example of B1 class'. The vessel is classified in D.L. Clarke's *Beaker Pottery of Great Britain and Ireland* as of Wessex/Middle Rhineland type, although it lacks the motifs usually associated with that group, being more akin to his All Over Corded Beakers. In his excavation report on Stockbridge Down, Stone begins to develop his theories about the cultural and ethnic origins of, and relationships among, the various peoples of prehistory as they related to Wessex.

The segmented faience bead Stone had discovered in the urnfield on Easton Down caused him to seek expert advice from H.C. Beck; together they wrote an article on the subject for *Archaeologia*. Faience was perhaps one of mankind's first attempts to produce an aesthetically pleasing synthetic material. It consists of a core of finely powdered grains of quartz, fired with alkali or lime, and covered with a surface glaze of soda-lime quartz glass coloured with salts of copper applied as a slip. It first appeared in Egypt in the third millennium BC, but did not appear in Europe until the second millennium BC. Stone's interest in the subject prompted him to take part in excavations in the Scilly Isles, County Wexford, Lough Gur in County Limerick, and the Aeolian Islands, where faience was discovered; he published journal reports on all four expeditions. The appearance of faience in Bronze Age Britain caused him to speculate on the routes taken by traders during the Bronze Age, and he concluded that Wessex was the focus of trade routes used for the exploitation of gold obtained from Ireland and lead from South Wales.

His expertise on faience beads led Stone to comment on similar finds from an excavation in Harappa, India. Using these beads he dated the site to 1550 BC on the basis of a spectroscopic analysis, showing that they had the same composition as similar beads, of known date, from Knossus. Then, in 1955, he was associated with an excavation at the Mound of Hostages at Tara in Ireland in which the first necklace containing faience was found in that country. It was similar to one that

Stone had examined earlier from North Moulton, in Devon. After the discovery of more faience in Ireland in 1956, he published a definitive paper on the use and distribution of faience, including its spectroscopic analysis. In his obituary to Marcus Stone, Professor Stuart Piggott wrote that:

> His work on glass and faience in Bronze Age Europe, using spectrographic analysis, is a fundamental contribution to our understanding of the critical contacts between the Aegean and Western Europe in the second millennium BC.

Durrington Walls was first identified as a major archaeological site in 1929 as a result of aerial photography, being recognised as a late Neolithic period or Early Bronze Age enclosure, some 0.5km in diameter. In 1951–2 a pipe trench 1m wide and 2m deep was cut through the site, a complete section 1km long thus being exposed. With Professor Stuart Piggott and A. St J. Booth, Stone undertook the examination of this lengthy section and performed further excavations that confirmed Durrington Walls as being built during what was then considered to be the second Neolithic phase, broadly contemporary with Woodhenge, which lay only 100m distant.

Stonehenge was to occupy Marcus Stone further. Such was his status that he was invited by the Ministry of Works, the then custodians of the monument, to join the foremost authorities on its archaeology, Stuart Piggott and Richard Atkinson, in an exploratory excavation there, and in supervising the raising of three of the fallen stones. In April 1952, they excavated Aubrey holes 31 and 32, animal bones being discovered in one hole and human bone in another, but no evidence was produced to indicate that the Aubrey holes had held posts or upright stones. Subsequent radiocarbon analysis of these remains produced dates of 2123–1573 BC (calibrated), corresponding to the end of the Neolithic period and the start of the Bronze Age.

Stone had invited John Musty to help in the Stonehenge excavations. Musty recounted that lunch was taken on one occasion in the encircling ditch, when Atkinson and Piggott enjoyed a bottle of wine. Marcus Stone appeared in his Morris Oxford car with a basket of strawberries and a bag of sugar that he always carried in the car. This was during the days of food rationing.

The *Wiltshire Archaeological and Natural History Magazine* for 1954 carried a review of the work by Atkinson, Piggott and Stone at Stonehenge, describing the evidence for a double circle of bluestones and their replacement by the familiar sarsens with their lintels, and the re-erection and supplementing of the bluestones in a new circle and a horseshoe arrangement. This interpretation remains the conventional one, although not unchallenged.

In 1952, Stone, along with David Algar, investigated a diffuse rubbish dump of Romano-British date on the Paul's Dene housing estate between Bishopsdown and Old Sarum, the site of *Sorbiodunum* – Roman Salisbury. Refuse including pottery, stone roofing tiles and coins was unearthed. The coins covered the period

18 Silver star marker for Ministry of Defence archaeological sites, designed by Marcus Stone

19 Marcus Stone's bookplate.
Courtesy Bourne Valley Historical Society

AD 69–405, and suggested to the excavators that the small town reached its peak of prosperity between AD 306 and AD 360.

Stone's final excavation, made with John Musty, was of an unrecorded Early Bronze Age barrow and urnfield on Heale Hill, Middle Woodford. Deep ploughing had thrown up sherds of Deverel-Rimbury pottery and investigation revealed that they came from a barrow. The primary interment was of an individual some 20 years old. The grave had been damaged by the insertion of two cinerary urns in the centre of the barrow. Three additional urns were found in close proximity to it.

Up to his sudden death, on 12 May 1957, Marcus Stone was fully active in archaeology. He was a founder member of the Bourne Valley Record and Historical Society in 1948, becoming its first President, and was a regular broadcaster of archaeological matters on the radio. He introduced the symbol of a silver star to mark archaeological monuments on the Porton Down Range (*18*), a method of marking which has since been extended to all Ministry of Defence archaeological sites to identify them to soldiers and ensure that they are not dug into. He became Chairman of the Committee of the Salisbury and South Wiltshire Museum. At the time of his death he had just completed the manuscript of a book, *Wessex before the Celts*, in which he summarised his lifetime of excavation and developed his ideas regarding the evolution of the different cultures in these islands. Fortunately, on Stone's death, Professor Stuart Piggott took charge of his manuscript and brought it to publication. It is still a readable and relevant volume; and even if after the passage of nearly half a century some of Stone's ideas regarding the flux of cultures by conquest and wholesale colonisation have been replaced by less dramatic notions of cultural diffusion, response to changing situations and absorbtive immigration, they stand as a rational and evolutionary attempt to explain and understand the complex issues involved.

Marcus Stone experienced good fortune during his life. He enjoyed a privileged education, a secure and well-paid job during the Depression years, and free range of a wonderland of archaeology. He benefited from an understanding management and a supportive wife. Fully conscious of his luck, and free from the time-consuming responsibilities of being a father, he got on with what interested him the most. He was eager to exploit new techniques: aerial photography, snail analysis, spectroscopy and thin-section microscopy. How he would have enjoyed radiocarbon dating! He encouraged all around him to share in, and contribute to, the study of archaeology and history. As a tribute to the monuments he worked on, he published all his work in the open literature – promptly. He is remembered for a kind and generous spirit.

One of Stone's many accomplishments was as an illustrator. He produced all his own drawings for publication. His view of himself and his life is well demonstrated by the personal bookplate he designed: two prehistoric men gazing with awe through lintelled uprights at Stonehenge towards the distant, dreaming spires of Oxford (*19*).

3

Chalk and flint:
geology and raw materials

The nature of a terrain's soil and its underlying rock formations determine the development of the natural flora and the use of the land by man, and hence have a bearing on the archaeological remains. The classification of chalk has recently undergone a radical change that has not yet been published in popular accounts, one that provides fresh insight into the distribution of the flint mines. It is worth considering the geology of Porton Down, if only briefly, for it will give an insight into the distribution of archaeology, in particular the flint mines and the settlements. Visitors to the flint mines have been interested in the processes of flint knapping. It is a technique that leaves a characteristic residue, but one that can be easily overlooked by the layman. For those reasons, the technology of flint knapping is briefly described in this chapter, too. Readers wishing to learn more about knapping should refer to Chris Butler's book *Prehistoric Flintwork*.

GEOLOGY

Chalk is composed of the compacted remains of countless billions of minute single-celled algae known as *coccolithophores* which live in seawater, from which they construct their hard shells using the calcium salts ever present in the oceans. When they die they fall to the ocean floor forming sediments of calcium carbonate, sometimes hundreds of metres thick, accumulating at a rate of about 2mm per millennium. When areas of the earth's crust buckle, owing to collisions of the tectonic plates, the chalk can rise above sea level where its contours become modified by erosion through the agencies of ice, frost, water in motion, and rainwater acidified with atmospheric carbon dioxide, often producing beautiful sculpted features, some of the best of which can readily be seen on the south scarps of the Marlborough Downs and the Vale of the White Horse. Cycles of upheaval and submersion can occur with the chalk becoming overlaid with sands, clays and gravels which themselves can get carried upwards with the chalk, or exposed through falling sea levels. These may, in turn, be scoured and redistributed by the agencies of erosion.

Other creatures inhabit the sea, some of which may tunnel into the layers of chalky sediment leaving burrow-shaped cavities. Some live and die upon the sea floor while others are free-swimming but die and fall to the sea floor where they, too, are covered by the ever present rain of *coccolithophores*. Many leave traces of themselves as their soft tissues rot, or are devoured by tiny carnivorous organisms, and their hard parts become fossilised. Some of the sea creatures, sea sponges especially, maintain their shape with internal skeletons in the form of spicules containing silica, the dioxide of the element silicon; these also form part of the sediments. Silica is one of the most common minerals on earth, the pure form of quartz. Over geological ages, and with help from acidified water, the silica can dissolve and percolate through the chalk where it fills the animal burrows and moulds, forming fossil remains. This silica solution also invades and replaces chalk along bedding planes, forming tabular flints, and also other cavities and burrows where it produces nodules of flint. Over time, some of the outer crystals of the silica become modified and combine with elements in the chalk to form a hard crust, called the cortex, more porous than the interior and whose white appearance results from the way it scatters light. The process is not entirely understood. Similarly, the faces of fractured flint on the surface absorb silica from the soil, becoming patinated, although the modern practice in archaeology is to refer to this process as cortication. The patina first takes on a blue colour in some humic soils, but it can be stained red by iron salts, especially from the weathering of pyrite, nodules of iron sulphide that formed in the chalk and which sometimes fancifully have been considered of meteoric origin and so gained the name 'thunderstones'. Such pyritic nodules have been discovered in archaeological contexts, functioning as strike-alights when struck with flint.

Chalk is not uniform in composition; the different layers were formed at different times and under various conditions. The fauna of the seas changed so that the several strata of the chalk contain groups of fossils specific to themselves, and which act as useful diagnostic aids for identifying particular layers. Slightly different conditions, under which flint formed, also led to the characteristic shapes and composition of the nodules. The chalk under our feet was laid down between 88 and 65 million years ago, during the last part of the Cretaceous period, and subsequently folded. At Porton Down, and also in the neighbourhood, the folding resulted only in a slight tilting of the strata so that the seams of flint within it are not quite horizontal. Then, the landscape was differentially eroded, leaving the plateaux and valleys seen today. Deposits of clay-with-flints overlying the chalk have been, as has been mentioned in Chapter 1, largely removed and redistributed, but remnants exist on Battery Hill and Tower Hill, and their round pebbles may be picked up almost anywhere. In some places the clay was deposited in holes and pipes in the chalk, where it remains. Clay has contributed to the formation of the humic soil, which technically belongs to the Icknield series.

The old classification into Lower, Middle and Upper Chalk Formations is no longer recommended for use by the British Geological Survey (BGS). For mapping purposes, the BGS has reclassified the old division of the Upper Chalk Formation into six distinct Members (a Member is a division of a Formation). A further reclassification has upgraded two of the three Members that outcrop on the Porton Range as Formations. Porton Down Range was surveyed in detail by Peter Hopson of the BGS in 1999, and the resulting map showing the different outcropping of the strata is given here (*20*). In ascending order these strata are the Seaford and Newhaven Chalk Formations and the Tarrant Chalk Member. Since the mapping was performed, the Tarrant Member has been defined as the lower part of the Culver Chalk Formation. For our purposes, it is sufficient to consider the outcropping chalk at Porton Down

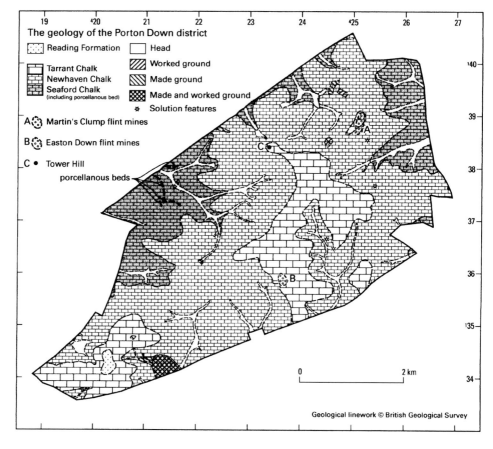

20 Map showing the distribution of chalk outcrops on the Porton Down Range. *Courtesy the British Geological Survey*

21 A selection of flint nodules from Porton Down. 1 Reading bed pebbles; 2 Small tabular
Newhaven tabular flint; 3 Tarrant flint nodules; 4 Newhaven flint nodules

as consisting of three different strata each possessing individual properties. I shall
adopt the obvious shorthand in referring to them. The Seaford Chalk outcrops in
the west of the Range, abutting the main railway line. Much of the remainder of
the Range is underlain by the Newhaven Chalk, with the Tarrant forming the caps
to hills and ridges and the higher plateaux.

Seaford Chalk is generally a firm to moderately hard, smooth, white chalk, with
numerous, regularly spaced nodular and tabular flint courses, with an extremely hard
capping, over which the plough merely skitters. Soil overlying this formation is rich
in worked flints, although it is doubtful whether the hard chalk would have been
mined in prehistory, when more easily worked layers were present. The inference
is that only naturally exposed flint nodules were worked in this deposit during
prehistoric times. Recently, Seaford Chalk has been used for building clunch walls.

The next layer, and most extensive at outcrop, is the Newhaven Chalk, a soft
chalk with few flints and these being mostly of small size and finger-like or spiky in
shape. These flints are generally unfit for fashioning into tools, or for use as building
material, but they find a modern use in manufacturing processes.

The uppermost layer at Porton Down, the Tarrant Chalk, is composed of material
with a hardness intermediate between the Seaford and the Newhaven Chalks. It
bears layers of tabular and nodular flint, familiar to everyone as the basic material of
flint-and-brick walling. Its flints are suitable for all knapping purposes (*21*) and most
prehistoric implements in the area were made from it.

FLINT KNAPPING

Flint is an ideal stone from which to fashion implements. It has no preferred plane of cleavage, which means that it can be worked in any direction equally well: one can create a scraper, say, either lengthwise or crosswise from the same nodule with equal expectations of success. It means, too, that for a percussive tool, an axe or an arrowhead for example, the ability to withstand shattering is independent of what direction the nodule, from which it originated, was worked. Flint was a valuable commodity, and although seemingly abundant in the landscape, flint nodules suitable for knapping tools on an industrial scale must be prospected and dug for. There are no thick seams of flint in Wiltshire as there at Grime's Graves in Norfolk where flint was also mined extensively during prehistoric times. The irregular nodules produced great amounts of waste material when knapped, so they were worked adjacent to the areas of extraction. By contrast, the grinding and polishing of flint axes could be performed equally well anywhere. The flint industry, therefore, implies a community settled for some period of the year, at least. Discoveries of dwelling sites and domestic pottery prove the point, although it is not yet clear whether tool manufacture was a full-time activity for some – a primary trade – or a seasonal one fitted to slack periods in the agricultural year. Whatever the situation, the knappers exhibit remarkable consistency of technique and considerable skill.

Some readers may be unfamiliar with flint flakes and cores. This section is intended as a general familiarisation. It does not attempt to be comprehensive and applies only to what has been discovered at Porton Down dating from the Neolithic period onwards.

Our ancestor *homo habilis* gained his name of 'handy man' from his ability to fashion stone tools half a million years ago. But even his primitive ancestors used the cutting properties of broken pebbles. When flint is broken it produces a cutting edge as sharp as finely honed surgical steel. We deal here with *homo sapiens*, 'wise man'; sometimes we need to remind ourselves that we are optimistically referring to ourselves. 'Modern man' (a much sounder epithet) includes our Neolithic forbears who were sophisticated beings and who, given the services of a tailor of modest abilities, a barber and a good scrubbing, would pass unnoticed among the stalls of Salisbury market on a Saturday morning, so long as they remained silent. This comparison is not meant to reflect adversely on the good folk of Salisbury, merely to counter a popular conception that Stone Age man was an uncouth and shambling creature, and that Stone Age woman was only marginally more refined.

A flint knapper would select a flint nodule, inevitably irregular in shape, and contemplatively or instinctively strike it with a hammer. A hammer might be another flint, most likely a pebble or even a fossilised sea urchin, a hard piece of wood or bone, or a piece of antler. In fine work, a soft hammer was preferable because it did not damage the flint at the point of impact. In crafts such as wood or stone working (but not always sculpting), the carpenter or mason seeks first to establish an initial flat surface from which to explore the third dimension. So it was, and is, with the flint knapper; his first blow created what we now call the 'striking platform' by detaching a flake of flint. With the removal of this flake the nodule becomes a 'core'. The knapper now struck the platform with blows aimed at right angles to it, significantly nearer the edge than the centre, with sufficient force to detach further flakes. It is easily imagined that considerable experience needs to be gained to achieve the desired result. The first flakes to be detached, ones whose outer surface is entirely covered with cortex, are termed primary flakes.

A typical detached flake bears the marks of being deliberately worked and is easily spotted by the trained eye even when it lies among flakes produced by weathering, the plough or indiscriminate shattering. At one end can be seen the flat remnant of the striking platform, lying roughly at right angles to the axis of the flake. Lying next to the remnant of the striking platform is the 'bulb of percussion', immediately below the point of impact (which may itself be observed if the hammer is a hard one). To one side of the bulb there may be a small 'bulbar scar' with short striations. On the face of the flake there are often 'conchoidal rings', ripples like those on a tranquil pond when the surface is disturbed at a point, the marks left by the shock wave of the blow as it travels through the flint, producing troughs and peaks of pressure within it. The bottom end of the flake where it left the core may be sharp; but in some instances the force of the blow, together with its point and angle of impact, may cause the end to display a 'hinge fracture', a smoothly rounded edge (which sometimes carries a little frill of flint), especially when the pattern of the pressure wave peaks there. It is unlikely that the flint knapper fully understood all these processes, but he or she could produce a better hand axe than we who can (*22*).

These are the main characteristics of a struck flint flake, although there are more and not all of them are present in every instance. We can now examine secondary and tertiary flakes. A secondary flake still bears traces of cortex, but both faces exhibit 'bare' flint. While one face carries the marks described above, the other displays a negative impression of the flake, or flakes, detached from it. Tertiary flakes bear no cortex. 'Thinning flakes' are produced at an advanced stage of production, for an obvious purpose, and 'pressure flakes' during the final preparation of an edge when applied pressure from a hard object removes small pieces of flint. All this waste, called 'debitage', is not to be confused with 'microliths', which are small flakes produced, mainly in the Mesolithic period, for delicate tasks or to set in numbers in hafts of wood or bone to produce saws and sickles.

Knappers produced 'core tools' or 'flake tools', although the word tool in this instance encompasses weapons and (certainly in modern times among virtuosos of knapping) ornaments where pleasing patterns of identical delicate flake scars are obligatory. One speaks of 'a core tool industry', although the term is used where flake tools are also made, because it carries the implication that core manufacture

22 Characteristics of worked flint flakes. 1 striking platform, bulb of percussion, bulbar scar and striations; 2 and 3 conchoidal rings; 4 flake scar; 5 crude scraper; 6 blade flake; 7 hinge fracture

is the more sophisticated and general process. Core tools, axes for example, are produced when flakes are detached from a nodule to shape the core into an implement. Flake tools like knives and scrapers are made from flakes detached for the purpose, or from serendipitous waste produced when working cores. Scrapers are made by fashioning them on a core and then detaching them with a single blow, with some subsequent edge working then undertaken. Edges of finished tools may be 'retouched' by removing additional flakes when they become worn. 'Microdenticulation' is performed when an edge is nicked several or many times per centimetre; such a tool acts like a steak knife.

4

The flint mines of Porton Down: the making of an industrial landscape

It is significant that all the known flint mines on the Porton Down Range are confined to the Tarrant Chalk, and the complexes peter out when, down-slope, they reach the Newhaven Chalk. The Tarrant is the only layer in which pits can be dug easily without collapse, and its flints are of good quality, of convenient shape and abundant. Sometimes it is conjectured that flint mines have an intensely ritual purpose, and that they were positioned on high ground so that their gleaming spoil heaps could act as conspicuous monuments. However, here the geological constraints mostly dictate that flint can only be mined successfully from the higher levels. It is also clear from excavations performed at Porton Down that spoil was deposited in nearby exhausted flint mines so that maximal use of the ground could be made. Heaps got in the way and were generally disposed of. Ritual no doubt attended flint mining, as deposits in flint mines affirm, particularly at Grime's Graves, but the evidence suggests that mining was conducted primarily to produce raw material for the utilitarian and economic production of tools and weapons, even if some of these spent their existence as status implements or cult objects. As I.F. Smith wrote over 30 years ago:

> …tools and weapons are basic equipment upon which survival depends and, within the limits of a stone technology, are likely to be closely adapted to the maintenance of a traditional mode of existence.

The importance of the study of flint working to our understanding of prehistory was also highlighted by Smith, who points out that the industry was homogenous across southern England, although associated with five or six different regional styles of pottery. The most basic common factor in prehistoric communities in Britain might therefore be found among the cultures clustered around the flint mines.

No longer is it generally accepted that the Neolithic period in the south began suddenly with the establishment of the Windmill Hill community north of Avebury. The desire to pin down an origin to a particular time and place is natural, but our evidence is only partial, unlike our eagerness to interpret, or to speculate. Peoples owning the cultural package usually associated with the Neolithic period – causewayed enclosures, large ritual monuments, long barrows, farming, distinctive pottery, and so forth – wrought sudden and dramatic changes in the landscape, and our earliest radiocarbon dates associated with such material occur in the few centuries immediately after 4000 BC. Accepting that production of the tools of existence were of immediate concern to society at the time, it is perhaps to the dating of flint mines that one should turn to assess when the Neolithic period in Britain 'began'. The radiocarbon date for an antler tine recovered from a Martin's Clump mine, 4230–4190 BC (BM-190, calibrated), is comparable, for example, to a date range of 4490–3810 BC (BM-181, calibrated) for the mines at Church Hill, West Sussex. Note, though, the uncertanties associated with reliance on a single radiocarbon estimate from a site that may possess a long history. Without the benefit of reliable dating techniques, Stone encountered difficulty in establishing the age of the Easton Down complex. He wrote:

> Estimates of the age of the mining period range from Palaeolithic to Early Bronze Age times. These have been derived mainly from the study of the forms of the implements found. As however Palaeolithic forms have repeatedly been found lying side by side with typical Neolithic celts [an antiquarian's name for an axe-like implement still in use by some archaeologists] in undisturbed floors in the four Sussex mines and in the present case, no other conclusion appears tenable than that *form alone is an unreliable criterion of age* [my italics].

In a later report on Easton Down, Stone quotes J. Reid Moir, a specialist in flint implements, commenting on a particular tool from the site:

> If such a thing was found in an ancient deposit, it would fit with its environment, but, the implement is a striking example of the survival of an archaic type into the Neolithic or even later times.

The single Easton Down calibrated radiocarbon date, 3630–2700 BC (BM-190, calibrated), comes from an antler pick recovered by Marcus Stone. His implicit conclusion was that the Easton Down mines were contemporary with the Beaker period settlement he discovered adjacent to them, and which is broadly datable from the pottery discovered there, an opinion that is not now tenable. Modern dating techniques show that the mines were earlier than the Beaker period settlements, but that does not preclude Beaker people having continued to extract flint from the site.

Barber *et al.*, in their *The Neolithic flint mines of England*, list only 10 certain prehistoric sites in England from which flint was mined using vertical shafts, and a further 10 possibles. The significance of having two major groups on the Porton Down Range is immediately apparent. These mines will now be discussed in detail.

THE FLINT MINES AT MARTIN'S CLUMP

The area known as Martin's Clump formed part of the same plateau of Tarrant Chalk as Easton Down in the geological past. The agencies of erosion have interposed a dramatic flat-bottomed dry coomb known locally as the Breck from its ecological similarity to the Brecklands of East Anglia. This sculpting, and the formation of the valley of the River Bourne to the north-west, has created a prominent ridge at Martin's Clump, which runs south-east to north-west and slopes gently eastwards into the Breck. A series of flint mines occupies the upper parts of this slope and extends almost to the summit of the ridge. Marcus Stone noted them in 1933 as slight depressions in the chalk and counted over 100 of them extending over 'some acres'. The ground there was covered with large flint flakes, and he picked up sherds of Beaker pottery from the surface. He discovered three workshop floors, one of which

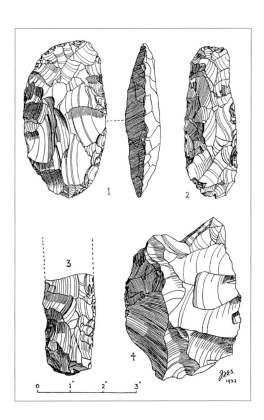

23 Worked flints from Martin's Clump drawn by Marcus Stone. *Courtesy WANHM*

he examined. It measured 8 x 4.3m and was 15cm thick, consisting of a mass of flint debitage containing broken and half-worked implements and pockets of tiny flakes. He illustrated four tools, one of which, numbered 1 in his illustration (*23*), is described as 'one of the best specimens of Palaeolithic form which has been found at either flint mine cluster'. This recurring desire on Stone's part to identify his tools with the Palaeolithic period, and the mines from which they derived, with both the Neolithic and Beaker periods is illogical and difficult to account for. As we shall discover, there are present-day so-called experts, who have probably never broken their fingernails in an excavation, who are willing to ignore provenance, patination and probability, hanging their reputations solely on the chancy hook of morphology.

The area at Martin's Clump had, in fact, been ploughed. A Tithe Apportionment of 1840 describes it wonderfully as 'Upper Down Field', an arable plot farmed by Joshua Brownjohn of Over Wallop. Further light ploughing at Martin's Clump occurred in the 1970s, within an area 200m² just to the north of the known area of flint mines in which an attempt was made to raise the great bustard, once native to Salisbury Plain. The author and his wife discovered and mapped a dense strip of mineshafts and spoil heaps lying between the northern edge of the bustard enclosure and a belt of woodland in 1989. Faint traces of shafts could be seen within the enclosure, and it became clear that the mined area was far more extensive than the marked area of known mines.

No evidence exists that Stone opened a flint mine at Martin's Clump, yet he wrote in his book, *Wessex before the Celts*, that '… the base of the pit was enlarged by undercutting to bell-shaped form at both Easton Down and Martins Clump'. The mystery remained until a chance encounter between David James of the Porton Down staff and Mrs Barbara Watson. Mrs Watson and her husband Major (later Lt Col) James Watson, who commanded a detachment of Royal Artillery at Porton Down, had excavated a mine at Martin's Clump during 1954–5 at the request of Marcus Stone. They had prepared a report on the excavation and submitted it to him, but it is now lost and searches for it have proved fruitless. Mrs Watson kindly agreed to be interviewed in 1986 and provided information on the dig from memory, and from notes written about the artefacts she had retained. She produced a collection of seven photographs of the excavation, one of which is shown (*24*). The mine appeared as a small depression before excavation and proved to be 2.5–3m deep and 3–3.5m in diameter, approximately circular with straight sides. A small 'gallery', one of Stone's 'undercuttings', about 1m high was found at the bottom of the shaft. It would appear to be part of the belling out process, which was not as smooth as Stone's cursory account of the site might suggest. An antler pick with a worn brow tine and a snapped off bez tine was discovered at a depth of 75cm, together with an isolated piece of antler. A discarded axe roughout 12 x 8.5cm was found at a depth of 1.5m, just above the gallery, with a quantity of charcoal which appeared to be the remains of a small fire. Two small axes were recovered.

24 The flint mine at Martin's Clump excavated by the Watsons. *Courtesy Mrs Barbara Watson*

An electricity cable trench was planned to cut the Quarley High Linear, a bank and ditch earthwork of the Iron Age running along the ridge at Martin's Clump, in 1984. It is a 'Scheduled Monument', listed by English Heritage who have agreed with the landowner to maintain conditions favourable to its preservation. In consequence of Scheduling, a section was excavated across it by hand by members of the Porton Down Conservation Group in advance of the mechanical digger. The excavation, which was reported in 1998, will be described fully in Chapter 6.

When the archaeological section had been completed, the mechanical digger extended the trench to skirt the known area of flint mines. In doing so it cut through four shafts lying outside the Scheduled area and not visible from the surface. The flint mines themselves were small, 1-2m in diameter. They were excavated only to the bottom of the cable trench, which was consistently 80cm deep. The trench probably grazed the sides of two more mines; one of these appeared as an ovoid area in the side of the trench, suggestive of a barrel-shaped shaft. Compared to the mine excavated by the Watsons lower down the slope, the ones on the ridge are small and probably shallow, and may not be representative of most of those at Martin's Clump. It is possible that the shafts cut by the cable trench belong to an early phase of mining and that extraction techniques changed over time.

The trench was continued down the slope, adjacent to the road, producing spoil rich in worked flints, until it came level with the eastern limit of the Scheduled area where the flint waste ceased to appear. This point coincided with the boundary of the Tarrant

Chalk, where it met the Newhaven. All the soil from the trench was laboriously sifted using a 100mm mesh sieve; 2,921 flint flakes and 16 cores were recovered, 610 of the flakes coming from a workshop floor lying adjacent to Flint Mine (FM) 1 (25), the spoil of which yielded 1,174 flakes, many of them very thin. Of a group of 60 flakes subsequently recovered from the interior of the shaft, 57 had no facets with cortex. It is likely, therefore, that the later, more delicate phases of knapping were performed within the shelter of the shallow or partially filled shaft. Local concentrations of flakes were discovered near two of the other mines cut through. Only one burnt flake was found.

A heavy, pointed tool 142mm long, resembling a hand axe and known technically as a 'ficron', was recovered from the spoil of the first mine (26). It was identified by British Museum staff as a Lower Palaeolithic tool, some 200,000 years old. Assuming this to be correct, it would have survived the last periglacial scouring, the only one known to have done so. In fact, its cortication matched that on all the other worked flint and it had emerged from a Neolithic hole. Other examples of the same Neolithic pattern have since been identified. Its form would have made it ideal for grubbing up roots, an essential activity in the Neolithic period when agriculture was expanding in response to an increasing population. The tool is superficially similar to known Palaeolithic forms, but it is surely an example of the convergence of design, where the pattern of a tool evolves to one best suited for its task, to whatever period it belongs, provided the skill and technology exist to produce it.

A crude, pointed tool, 119mm in length, was recovered from the spoil of one shaft, very similar to one from Easton Down illustrated by Stone and described by him as a rostro-carinate hand axe. The nodule from which it was manufactured contained a large and obvious flaw. Its appearance suggests an apprentice piece, contrasting vividly with the exceptionally fine workmanship of the ficron. Some delicate flakes were present in the lithic assemblage; one showed definite evidence of further working. This flake, 46mm long, exhibited microdenticulation along one edge, 23 dentils per 10mm of edge at one stretch. One large, long, crudely knapped flint with an apparently worn tip is thought to be a wedge for use during flint mining operations.

The only ceramic discovered was a single shard of Beaker ware of later date in the spoil from a shaft. It probably came from the base of the disturbed humic layer. From the same spoil were also recovered part of a sheep or goat tibia with gnaw marks consistent with chewing by a dog; part of a cow femur; and part of an antler – a brow, bez or trez tine from a red deer – displaying wear on the tip. A similar antler tine was recovered from the wall of the trench through one shaft. This was submitted for radiocarbon dating, resulting in the range of dates quoted above. A cow's limb bone, 153mm long, was recovered from the spoil of the same mine which also contained a fragment of bone 61mm long, displaying an oblique cut 14mm long as if caused by butchery with a knife. Thirteen species of molluscs were extracted from 1kg of soil taken from FM1, 80cm below the surface; the presence of *Vertigo pusilla* indicates a well-drained environment, such as is expected on high chalk downland.

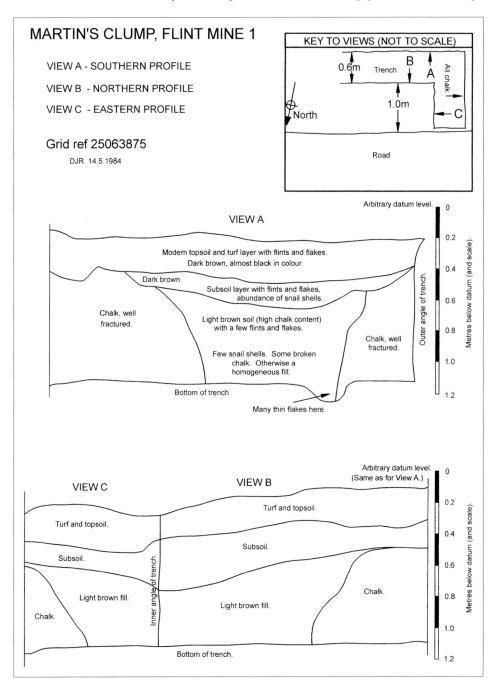

MARTIN'S CLUMP, FLINT MINE 1

VIEW A - SOUTHERN PROFILE

VIEW B - NORTHERN PROFILE

VIEW C - EASTERN PROFILE

Grid ref 25063875

DJR 14.5.1984

KEY TO VIEWS (NOT TO SCALE)

0.6m   Trench   B   A   All chalk

1.0m   C

North

Road

Arbitrary datum level.   0

VIEW A

Modern topsoil and turf layer with flints and flakes.
Dark brown, almost black in colour.

Dark brown.

Subsoil layer with flints and flakes,
abundance of snail shells.

Chalk, well
fractured.

Light brown soil (high chalk content)
with a few flints and flakes.

Chalk, well
fractured.

Few snail shells. Some broken
chalk. Otherwise a
homogeneous fill.

Bottom of trench.

Many thin flakes here.

Outer angle of trench.

Metres below datum (and scale).

0.2
0.4
0.6
0.8
1.0
1.2

Arbitrary datum level.   0
(Same as for View A.)

VIEW C   VIEW B

Turf and topsoil.

Turf and topsoil.

Subsoil.

Subsoil.

Light brown fill.

Light brown fill.

Chalk.

Chalk.

Inner angle of trench.

Bottom of trench.

Metres below datum (and scale).

0.2
0.4
0.6
0.8
1.0
1.2

25 Profiles of Flint Mine 1 at Martin's Clump

0   10 CM

26 The ficron from Martin's Clump

Too few tools were recovered in 1984 to make a comparison with Easton Down, but they may be aggregated with those recovered by Stone and those located from the Watsons' dig. The Martin's Clump assemblage is, then, not significantly different from that obtained from Easton Down. Imperfect, discarded tools are more likely to be discovered in a manufacturing context, although there is no reason to suppose that their distribution is unrepresentative of the complete toolkit.

A flat, ovoid sandstone axe was discovered driven into the ground close to the linear feature. It is clearly a modified beach pebble. Similarly shaped pebbles occur at the tide level at Dunster in north Somerset and no doubt elsewhere too. The working edge had been pecked and ground into shape, and it bears wear marks consistent with being set into a haft. In view of the Cornish axe discovered at Porton, an expert opinion was sought from Dr R.W. Sanderson of the British Museum's Department of Minerology, who concluded that it was probably a 'one off' tool, made locally. Its hard nature suggests it derived from Palaeozoic strata, resembling stone from the Old Red Sandstone of the Devonian or Upper Carboniferous strata of the borders of north Devon, but its durability leads to specimens of the rock being found as erratic fragments throughout southern England, presumably having been transported by glacial or river activity. However, it seems more plausible that it was selected from a beach, for only a few of the pebbles at Dunster are of exactly the right shape and size to turn into axes. Rivers and glaciers don't perform this type of selection. Michael Pitts, in a lengthy

Proceedings of the Prehistoric Society article in 1996, has reviewed stone axes, including flint ones, but no modified beach pebbles were included in his analysis, so the rarity of the Porton specimen cannot be gauged. There are no indications as to its date.

The activity at Martin's Clump, and the interest it aroused, encouraged the RCHME (the Royal Commission on the Historical Monuments of England, now part of English Heritage), who were undertaking an investigation into Neolithic Enclosure and Industry in England, to survey the flint mines there (*27*) after realising that the site was far more extensive than had been imagined. The mined area proved to be 4.5 hectares in extent, with flint extraction surviving as shallow surface depressions with occasional spoil heaps. Ploughing had reduced and rounded their profiles to no more than 20cm in height. Three hundred and fify-seven shafts were recorded, mostly small in diameter, but larger than those reported by the author, being 4m to 5m across, although the largest are *c*.8m in diameter. In five instances shafts appear to be conjoined. In places they occurred in clusters, particularly to the south-west and north-east of the bustard pen. Within the penning, identifiable depressions were more isolated, probably reflecting the recent ploughing. Simple

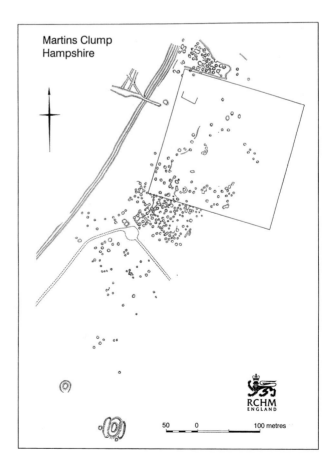

27 RCHME's survey of the flint mines at Martin's Clump, and the oval barrow. © *Crown Copyright. NMR*

extrapolation, multiplying the density of the mines where they can be identified with most certainty by the area in which they occur, leads to an estimate of some 1,000 shafts having been dug. This figure would make Martin's Clump the largest flint mine complex in England, although it is no bigger than Grime's Graves in extent, and was probably far less productive than the Norfolk mines owing to the inferior nature of the flint deposits.

As noted, there is an increasing conviction among archaeologists that ritual practices played a large part in the placing and operating of prehistoric flint mines. The arguments include appeals to ethnological parallels and unnecessary mining where more easily obtained flint exists nearby. The occurrence of ritual deposits in Grime's Graves and elsewhere has been noted, but these may have been more the superstitious actions of individual miners concerned for their own safety than products of a communal belief or a ceremony. Stone linked his cephalotaphic barrow with the ritually expressed concern of a community for their well being, and a barrow is almost certainly the product of group effort. Some sense of reverence for, or acknowledgement of, the past is certainly displayed by the builders of the urnfield at Easton Down who located it at the edge of the much earlier flint diggings.

However, there is a parallel instance of such placement at Martin's Clump. On the easternmost limit of the flint mines there, overlooking the Breck, lies a long barrow, ovoid in plan, orientated north-north-east to south-south-west, 36m long and some 27m wide at the centre, where it rises 2m above the surrounding ditches (*27*). Another such barrow lies 1.5km to the east. These features are not the familiar Neolithic long barrows, either earthen or chambered, but intermediate in form between the true Neolithic long barrow and the round barrows of the Bronze Age. They are better described as oval barrows, and it is tempting to speculate that they are intermediate in date between the two periods. The placement goes further: a round barrow impinges on the southern ditch of the long barrow, and a second round barrow lies some 100m north of it. Although rodent damage has obscured the sequence of the building of these monuments, it seems most probable that the long barrow came first. Both the urnfield and the long barrow appear constrained by notions of 'the boundary', for such ideas of liminality are recurrent throughout many cultures. This may be true of the round barrows, too. One barrow may be independently observing a perceived boundary of ancient earthworks; the other seems to be concerned more with an identification with the long barrow, its liminal connection deriving by proxy from it, another acknowledgement of 'the ancestors' perhaps.

These instances of ritual practice at Porton Down are unconnected with the physical processes of flint extraction. The shafts are limited to areas of good quality flint nodules, their placement must therefore be assumed to be entirely due to practical considerations.

THE FLINT MINES AT EASTON DOWN

One ponders what the ancient shepherds who wandered Easton Down made of the humps and depressions in the ground. Farmers of Napoleonic times were conscious of them, for they ploughed round them as inconveniences. Marcus Stone discovered the site, as we noted, by observing trackways and ditches converging on the area. Again, his conclusion was that these features were directly related to the flint mines. In his first report, he stated his intention to publish 'the mass of information' he obtained on the linear features, but he never did.

The mined area lies at the head of a narrow, shallow coomb that was covered with scrub in 1929. An estate map of 1812 for the Manor of East Winterslow shows the mined area as under pasture; land to the east of a north–south linear feature, where Stone would later discover 'a Beaker Period Settlement', is shown as under cultivation. A Tithe Award map of 1843 shows the site as lying within pasturelands, with the area to the north of them as arable. Stone's interest in the site was kindled by the masses of waste flint flakes and broken implements lying on the surface and in rabbit scrapes. He identified 90 roughly circular surface depressions, although

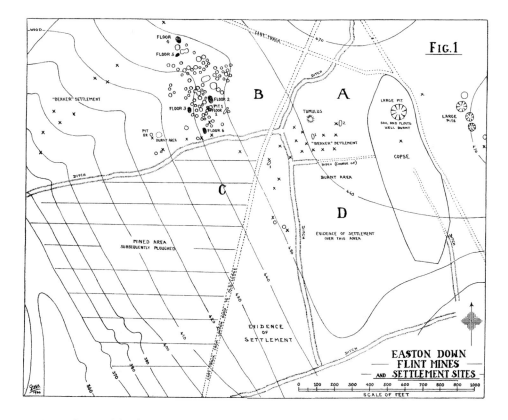

28 Original map of the flint mines at Easton Down. *Courtesy WANHM*

he considered that many more had been levelled by the plough, particularly to the south. The depressions were mapped by Mr J. Cochrane-Houston (*28*). The map shows two linear earthworks that divide the area into quadrants, designated A, B C and D. The depressions lie in the north-western quadrant, B.

Excavations commenced in 1929, with a small, shallow depression, 4.3m in diameter and 15cm deep. It had no adjacent spoil heap to hinder the work and there was no sign of rabbit disturbance, unlike many of the shafts. The shaft was sectioned to a depth of 1.8m. The top of the section was removed, then excavation continued to the bottom, a depth of 3.6m (*29*). The shaft had obviously been refilled with its own or another's spoil, which consisted of blocks of chalk – some of which bore the marks of antler picks. The shaft had penetrated two layers of poor quality tabular flint to reach what Stone called the floorstone, taking the terminology from Grime's Graves where the shafts reached a thick seam of nodular flint. Tabular flint from the shaft, or its neighbour, had been thrown back into it, too. In this fill there were animal remains consisting of the sur-royal tines from a red deer antler, identified as a rake, and the broken scapula of an ox used for a shovel. Three knapped tools were recovered from this infill.

Covering the main filling there was a layer of chalky silt 30cm thick containing worked flint waste that had washed down from a workshop floor located next to the shaft. Above this silt was a layer of brown 'rainwash' 60cm thick containing numerous

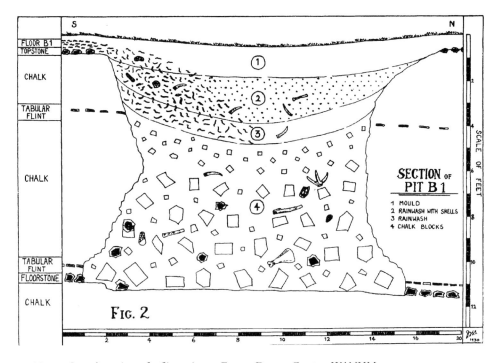

29 Marcus Stone's section of a flint mine at Easton Down. *Courtesy WANHM*

waste flakes, some animal bones and several flint implements, including an adze, some 'choppers' and a scraper. Numerous shells from land molluscs were extracted from the layers, and passed for analysis to A.S. Kennard. This type of analysis was to become standard practice. The humic layer at the top of the shaft contained masses of large flakes, a 'celt-like tool' and a tool similar to a Palaeolithic hand axe. Waste flakes in the uppermost layers were most numerous on the south side, and this is where a 'workshop floor' was found, an area where knapping had occurred. It measured 5.5 x 7.3m and was no more than 25cm deep, and was composed of a compact mass of flakes, roughed out implements and finished tools. 'Two nests of the minutest of flakes were found, one at each end of the floor, presumably where the finished touches were given.' At least eight implements were recovered, four of which are illustrated in below (*30*), one of the most interesting is the waisted tranchet axe (Stone's Figure 1). Similar tools were found in the flints of a cairn at Easton Down, discussed in the next chapter, and on Tower Hill.

Another workshop floor, similar to the first and containing further implements, was discovered in an area to the north-west, near to Pit B1 on the map. Here lay the waste from a gunflint industry, perhaps only 200 years old. Gunflint knappers had discovered a rich source of raw material in the Neolithic flint residue.

A small depression 1.8m in diameter lay beneath the workshop floor, and this was excavated. Beneath a 'sterile layer of mould' lay another layer rich in molluscan

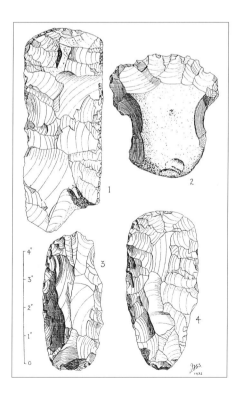

30 Worked flints from Easton Down, including a waisted tranchet axe. *Courtesy WANHM*

shells; there were some flakes and fragments of tools, the skull and teeth of a dog and also two broken antler tines. Lower still, was a 45cm-thick layer of black flakes, implements and large nodules of floorstone. At this level a narrower pit, 60cm in diameter, had been dug to a depth of 60cm in the base of the shaft. It was filled with chalk. The pit had not penetrated or reached any significant flint layer and was considered to be unfinished or abandoned.

Two more workshop floors were discovered, both comprising of masses of flint flakes, 'roughouts' and implements. One measured 5.5 x 2.7m and was in the form of a figure-of-eight. One loop was composed entirely of flakes while the other was formed from much smaller chippings with three implements buried in them. Both were prolific for implements, with one containing a nest of minute flakes. One tool was described as 'a hand axe of Drift form', that is of Palaeolithic type. It is interesting that so many of these Neolithic tools appeared to Stone to be of Palaeolithic pattern. They must be examples of the convergence of design discussed above.

The next tranche of work on Easton Down was published in 1933 and describes the excavation of four more mineshafts and two more workshop floors. The largest pit had an encircling bank of spoil and measured 8m from bank to bank, with the top of the shaft 5m in diameter. Here the flint seam appeared at a depth of 2.4m where undercutting occurred in four places to produce a greatest diameter of 6m. A second shaft had been sunk in the productive floor of the shaft, enabling Stone to link the mine with those at Harrow Hill and Cissbury, both in Sussex, where similar double working had been noted, although the secondary shaft at Easton Down had not encountered any flint. Its main fill contained a few tools, six scapulae from oxen, three of them identified as wild oxen, and three broken antlers. Three more almost perfect antlers were discovered in contact with the flint layers; their tines had been broken off and were embedded in the chalk face, proving their function. Two antlers had been charred in a fire, and a heap of charcoal lay nearby, originating from either hazel or alder, and ash wood. It was one of these antlers that provided the sole radiocarbon date for the mines. None of the other three pits examined had reached flint. Stone was particularly interested in the workshop floors because he thought they would provide evidence for dating from the pattern of the implements that were most abundant there, although this belief stands in strong contradiction to his realisation that tool types were similar to those known to span a vast period.

On the eastern edge of the map of the mines are marked some very large pits. There are no spoil heaps round them and they are considered to be natural solution holes (of which other examples exist at Porton Down) where cavities have formed in the underlying chalk and collapse has occurred. However, the soil within the largest natural pit has a huge component of crushed burnt flint, an archaeological phenomenon as yet unexplained.

The Easton Down site was resurveyed in 1979 by RCHME, and was reassessed by them in 1998. The survey identified 70 depressions, only a few of which could be matched with those numbered on the original map. Stone's belief that more mines had been ploughed out in his Area C was not substantiated by the new survey, which also re-evaluated the evidence for the settlement sites. The survey was also valuable for its consideration of other archaeological features in the immediate landscape, and we shall return to it in Chapter 5.

THE FLINT EXTRACTION AND KNAPPING ON TOWER HILL

Tower Hill is so named after an early eighteenth-century tower, or folly, that once crowned its crest. Encircling the hilltop is an apparent low bank and associated ditch. The site was topographically surveyed in 1998 by RCHME (*31*); simultaneously a resistivity survey was conducted by Henry Stevens of the University of Southampton. The primary interest lay in investigating the remains of the folly, which will feature in Chapter 8. However, the slopes of the folly are liberally scattered with prehistoric flint flakes, and a preliminary assessment of 57 of these ascribed the bulk to the early Neolithic period. The topographical survey emphasised the existence of the bank and ditch but did not answer questions regarding its origin. It could be a garden boundary,

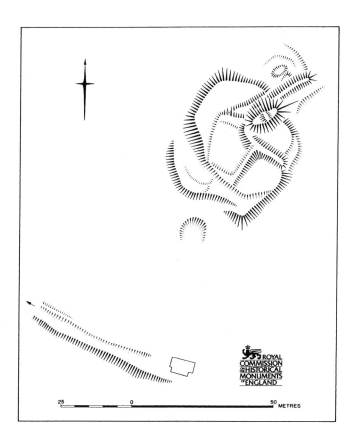

31 RCHME's topographical survey of Tower Hill. © *Crown Copyright. NMR*

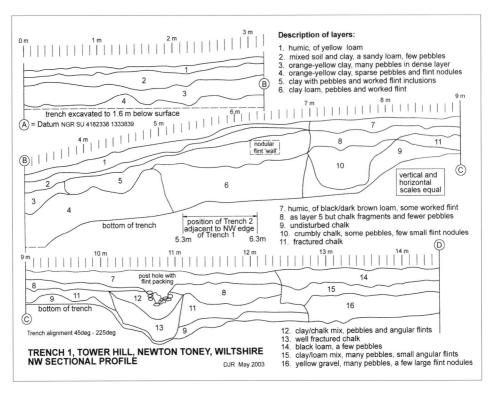

Description of layers:

1. humic, of yellow loam
2. mixed soil and clay, a sandy loam, few pebbles
3. orange-yellow clay, many pebbles in dense layer
4. orange-yellow clay, sparse pebbles and flint nodules
5. clay with pebbles and worked flint inclusions
6. clay loam, pebbles and worked flint

7. humic, of black/dark brown loam, some worked flint
8. as layer 5 but chalk fragments and fewer pebbles
9. undisturbed chalk
10. crumbly chalk, some pebbles, few small flint nodules
11. fractured chalk

12. clay/chalk mix, pebbles and angular flints
13. well fractured chalk
14. black loam, a few pebbles
15. clay/loam mix, many pebbles, small angular flints
16. yellow gravel, many pebbles, a few large flint nodules

trench excavated to 1.6 m below surface
Ⓐ = Datum NGR SU 4182338 1333839

nodular flint 'wall'

vertical and horizontal scales equal

bottom of trench

position of Trench 2 adjacent to NW edge of Trench 1
5.3m   6.3m

post hole with flint packing

bottom of trench

Trench alignment 45deg - 225deg

**TRENCH 1, TOWER HILL, NEWTON TONEY, WILTSHIRE
NW SECTIONAL PROFILE**   DJR May 2003

32 Profile of Trench 1, Tower Hill

for garden features are known to be associated with follies and were identified by the survey; alternatively it could represent a hitherto unrecognised prehistoric hilltop enclosure. The Porton Down Conservation Group undertook a simple linear excavation across the feature to make the determination, and published the results in 2005.

A trench 14.5m long and 1m wide was excavated by hand (*32*). The lower part of the trench was sectioned, to a depth of 1.6m and the putative ditch, which turned out to cross a deposit of stiff, orange clay of the Reading beds with their characteristic ovoid pebbles – although the deposit here also included flint nodules – was an example of the aptly named 'clay-with-flints'. Most pebbles were small, typically below 30mm in length, although some isolated specimens exceeded 200mm. The deposit consists of sediments laid down early in the Tertiary period, perhaps 25 million years ago, and redistributed in a solution hole in the chalk sometime after 1.6 million years ago, when the flints were mixed with it. The pebbles were more or less evenly spread throughout the bulk of the material, but gradual top-down erosion of the clay over geological periods has resulted in a denser layer of pebbles near the surface. This pebble layer had not been breached in the region of the 'ditch', clearly showing that it was not a man-made feature but of geological origin. However, further upslope the pebble layer had been disturbed. Material in the section was mixed with pebbles and worked flint flakes and cores. The appearance was of a filled-in depression or pit, 2m wide, that cut through the Reading beds, with extensive knapping activity on top of it. Further upslope, large flint nodules, many of them cores, had been carefully laid together to form a low wall, step or revetment, some 30cm wide by 20cm deep. The pit or scrape was separated from another probable pit by a few centimetres. This second pit appeared shallow, but this aspect may have been presented by the trench cutting the edge of a deeper, tapering feature. Beyond this pit, which contained only broken chalk and a few flint nodules, the ground remained undisturbed for a further 2m. Then there appeared in the section a collection of large flint nodules, interpreted as packing around a substantial post. Another small trench, Trench 2, was excavated to a depth of 40cm adjacent to the northern edge of the area where the 'revetment' was observed. This excavation confirmed the continuation of the flint packing and produced many more flint flakes and some cores, which disappeared abruptly from the section at a depth of 40cm.

The excavation showed that, at the position of the trench, at least, the indication for an encircling bank and ditch could be attributed to a depressed geological feature – a clay-filled solution hole in the chalk – and to an elevated line of deliberately placed flint nodules upslope of it which produced a pronounced scarp. How far this arrangement can be extrapolated round the hill is unclear, but it was plain that the top of the hill was composed of Tarrant Chalk, and from flint nodules in surface scatters and rabbit burrow spoils lower down, that the Newhaven Chalk outcropped there. Generally, there is a clear break of slope between the two types of chalk, implying that the 'enclosure' revealed by the topographical plan could be, at least partially, an artefact of geology. However, the building of the folly and its gardens (or landscaping) involved much disturbance of the soil, so the nature of the earthwork was not determined by a simple sectioning of it at one point, as was hoped for.

Flint 'mining' on Tower Hill was not a process of digging neat round pits, as on the plateaux to the east and the south. If a knapper can obtain his raw material without too much effort from where horizontal seams of nodules outcrop on hillsides, he will almost certainly do so. But having recourse to these, and having exploited them, what does he do next? The probability is that he would dig down a little, forming an untidy quarry. This imagined activity exactly matches the jumbled stratification encountered in the trench.

The analysis of the worked flint found in the excavation is described in some detail here because it demonstrates to the reader how the evidence can be evaluated and opinions formed. By professional standards it is a very simple analysis, and so easily understood. (A seminal example of a professional analysis is that by Dr Frances Healy in the *Proceedings of the Prehistoric Society*, Volume 58.)

Trench 1 yielded 3,001 flint flakes, totalling 24.41kg in weight. The 25 cores weighed 2.36kg. From Trench 2, 1,185 flakes and 21 cores were obtained (9.92kg and 1.68kg in weight, respectively). Some of these flakes are illustrated (*33*). One prismatic core 60mm in length was recovered, a quasi-cylindrical flint bearing the circumferential scars of flakes detached longitudinally, typical of the Mesolithic period but also of the Early Neolithic. Forty-eight complete blade flakes (length to breadth ratio exceeding 3:1) were recovered, including delicate blade flakes, typically 25 x 5mm, consistent with the pattern of flake scars on the prismatic core. In total, 15 tools were found: four awls or borers; four scrapers; six fabricators of different patterns; and a waisted tool 90mm long discovered in the upper layers of the 'ditch', away from the main knapping area, which suggests a different period of manufacture. There were also six flakes with obvious notches. Although blade flakes similar to those struck in the Mesolithic period, and considered to be diagnostic, were present, they occurred in such small numbers, 2.7 per cent of all tertiary flakes (those with no cortex on them), that the assemblage was deemed to be later than the Mesolithic period. The function of the waisted tool is uncertain; it could have been used to remove bark from wooden rods, such as arrows or hafts. It is of a pattern found throughout the Neolithic, and is practically identical to one in Martin Green's collection from Cranborne Chase, even down to the distribution of the cortex, and similar to one discovered by Stone at Easton Down. Thus, on Tower Hill, we can tentatively conclude that flint extraction and knapping occurred intermittently over many hundreds of years, possibly beginning in the Mesolithic period but certainly occurring in the Neolithic and Early Bronze Age.

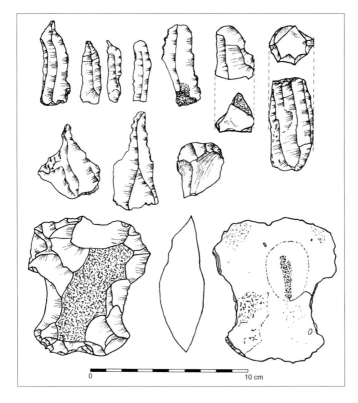

33 Prehistoric worked flints from Tower Hill

OTHER FLINT MINES

A. St J. Booth and Marcus Stone wrote in *The Wiltshire Archaeological Magazine* for 1954:

> When we take into account the density of Neolithic and Early Bronze Age occupation of the flint-bearing chalk downs of Wiltshire, and of the known dependence of the period on flint for tool and implement manufacture, [the] short list of recognised mines seems scarcely impressive.

The authors were describing six 'trial' flint mines lying between Woodhenge and Durrington Walls, dated to the late Neolithic period that only came to light after being cut by a sewerage trench in 1952, but the observation has general relevance.

One can recover worked flint from the ploughsoil almost anywhere on the chalk downland, not just on the mined areas. This suggests that surface flint was knapped, although it would not have been of the best quality having undergone many frosting cycles. But surface scatters of nodules were an insufficient supply for the vast numbers of flakes and flints that were produced over many hundreds of years. It appears that the small number of known flint mines would not have satisfied the demand, either, leading to the supposition that many more have not been discovered. These may have consisted of small groups of shafts, easily overlooked after disturbance of the ground, as at Durrington. The power of the plough to obliterate them can be seen at Martin's Clump, where one pass of a light plough significantly reduced the apparent density of them compared to their neighbours. Had not Porton Down been enclosed they, and perhaps the Easton Down group, would probably have been obliterated by agriculture also.

Close to the centre of Porton village, next to the River Bourne, lies a field obviously used as a quarry in historic times for the extraction of building flint and chalk for cob. Apparently, and logically, exploitation began at the bottom of the sloping field and nearest the track leading to its access. Quarrying stopped before the upper part of the field had been worked, and here lies a circular depression very similar to those at Easton Down, a mere 4.5km to the east. Prehistoric flint flakes are abundant in the field, and a scraper and a fabricator have been recovered. It is almost certain that the field, lying so near to the farm to which it belonged, was not used for agriculture in medieval times because of its pitted and rutted surface resulting from prehistoric activity, and was subsequently only deemed fit for use as a quarry. If such an obvious feature has only recently been recognised for what it is, there could be many more flint mines awaiting discovery on the chalk lands.

5

Dwellings for the living, houses for the dead

Following the Neolithic period, a new culture spread across Europe. In Britain it began around 2500 BC and was marked by a notable increase in sophistication in ceramics, jewellery, weapons and monuments. The culture takes its name from its finely made Beakers, produced in a variety of forms of which the most instantly recognisable is the bell-shaped vessel with a waist. They were usually decorated, some with impressed twisted cords, others with exquisitely worked geometrical patterns executed with a stylus – often a bird's bone or a fingernail. Gold began to appear in jewellery and as embellishments to personal weapons, the latter being fashioned initially from copper but then, around 2000 BC, from the harder bronze – copper alloyed with a small percentage of tin, often around 13 per cent.

These riches speak of a hierarchical society, a point confirmed by the discovery of the 'Amesbury Archer' in 2001 during archaeological exploration in advance of the building of a school. Members of Wessex Archaeology were nearing the end of their investigation of a Romano-British cemetery, but had a few features left to examine, one of which yielded Beaker pottery. A rare gold adornment, thought to be an earring or a hair adornment, was unearthed, the precursor to the discovery of a fabulous treasure, the most sumptuous group of grave goods found in a Beaker burial in England, indeed, in Europe. They marked the body out as a man of rank, possibly the highest, with the accoutrements of an archer and a metal worker. How fascinating it was to discover the status accorded to a crafter of precious metals, even if it was an honorary compliment! And like all mythical smiths he was lame: his left leg was withered. He wore an archer's sandstone wrist guard and was festooned with 15 finely knapped flint arrowheads, and had beside him three antler tools for working flint. He carried a Spanish copper knife; two other copper knives lay nearby. Bone pins and boars' tusks suggested adornment. Four Beaker vessels surrounded him. Analysis of his teeth showed high levels of an oxygen isotope; contour maps of isotopic values suggest that 'the King of Stonehenge' grew up near the Alps. Radiocarbon analysis of his bones yields a calibrated date range 2400–2200 BC.

It was within this date range, or slightly later, that the sarsen stones were erected inside the Neolithic earthen circle of Stonehenge.

ROUND BARROWS

The Early Bronze Age is commonly associated with rich burials beneath large round barrows. A good example being the famous Bush Barrow near Stonehenge, decorated with tiny gold pins and two gold lozenge plates. But the example of the Amesbury Archer shows that important graves were not always covered by large mounds, and numerous 'crouched Beaker burials' lacked covering mounds. The Bush Barrow gave rise to the notion of a Wessex Culture of rich chieftains, but Anne Woodward argues in her *British Barrows* that it was an uncharacteristic burial. Not all barrows cover or contain burials, but sufficient numbers of them did to encourage the barrow diggers of the eighteenth and nineteenth centuries to search them for treasure.

A large-scale, systematic, aerial photographic survey of the Porton Down Range was conducted for mapping purposes in November 1984. The elements conspired to produce a tool of great value to the archaeologists: the lighting was optimal, the soil moisture content was ideal and the vegetation at its most revealing. In the ploughsoil there appeared the long ploughed-out remains of barrows, Celtic fields and linear features, some new to sites and monuments records. Ancient furrow marks appeared. Even on the swarded areas, known features could now be mapped with ease. The photographic appraisal aided a ground survey of all the barrows on the Porton Down Range conducted by Martin Papworth for the then Trust for Wessex Archaeology in 1984-5, which formed part of a southern counties project, specifically to identify unprotected barrows in good condition and possessing the potential for archaeological study. Barrows were, and are, being destroyed at an alarming rate by agriculture and suffer cumulative massive damage from rabbits.

The structure, dimensions, burials and contents of round barrows vary widely. Burials could be single or multiple inhumations, cremated remains, sometimes in urns, or insertions into an old barrow. One classification useful for cataloguing Bronze Age round barrows in the landscape is by type: bowl, bell, disc, saucer and pond (*34*). All are represented at Porton Down. The majority are bowl barrows, typically a small mound surrounded by a ditch and sometimes an outer bank. The bell barrow has a large mound separated from a ditch by a 'berm', or platform. The warrior equipment and rich grave goods, if present, is often thought to signify the burial of a warrior. The disc barrow has a proportionately smaller central mound than the bell barrow. Finds of jewellery and domestic implements have been used to support the assumption that disc barrows are the graves of women. The saucer

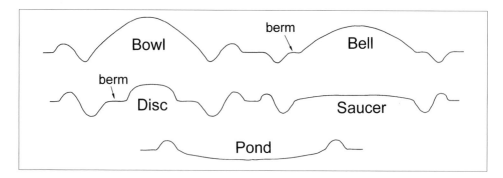

34 General profiles of some round barrows

barrow has a low mound covering the whole circle within the ditch and outer bank. Few barrows of this type have been excavated. The pond barrow comprises a circular depression surrounded by an outer bank. Its association with barrow groups suggests that it was not sepulchral but was connected with funerary ritual.

The Papworth survey identified a total of 106 barrows, two of them of the oval barrow variety, a form associated with the Neolithic period; the rest of them were Bronze Age round barrows. Excavation records, many sketchy, exist for 22 of them, but nineteenth-century prospectors damaged many more without leaving accounts of their activities. At the time of the survey there were 11 unploughed barrows in ploughed fields, 11 barrows in woodland and 45 barrows on rough grass. The remainder were ploughed over or built upon. The report identified the barrow cemetery on Idmiston Down as particularly worthy of preservation. It includes five bowl barrows, an unusual bowl with an external bank, two disc barrows and a large bell barrow.

Other important barrow cemeteries exist on the Porton Down Range, particularly at New Plantation and the Winterslow Hut group (*13*), which has already been mentioned in connection with the excavations conducted by the Rev A.B. Hutchins in 1814. The primary burial in Hutchins's 'bell barrow of chalk', number three in *Figure 13*, consisted of a crouched skeleton with a beaker accompanied by a bronze dagger, two tanged flint arrowheads and a slate wrist guard. Above this lay a secondary burial of a few bones in a Middle Bronze Age urn, above which a further secondary burial, of the Late Bronze Age, had been made, of a cremation burial in an urn, the ashes of which had been wrapped in linen. Also present in the urn were a bronze awl, a bronze razor and a pygmy cup containing hairs, identified as numerous eyebrows. Hutchins opened a nearby barrow, his 'colossal barrow', number 23 in *Figure 13*, in which he discovered a Saxon secondary burial of a large skeleton with an iron shield boss and handgrip, spearhead, buckle and a wooden bucket hooped with bronze. Hutchins penetrated no further than the secondary burial, intending to return to complete the barrow's examination at a future date. Finds from the barrows are the subjects of the two paintings by Thomas Guest (*35* and *colour plate 9*).

35 Oil painting by Thomas Guest of finds from Rev Hutchins' excavation of a round barrow (number 23) in the Winterslow Hut group. *Courtesy Salisbury Museum*

The largest barrow in the group, the Winterslow Great Barrow (*colour plate 11*), a bowl thought to be the largest in Wiltshire, is reported as unexcavated, although there is a suspicious-looking depression in the top. The mound is 5.5m in height with a diameter of 32m, and is estimated to contain 750 cubic metres of chalk. It probably took a similar number of men days to complete. A linear feature respects the barrow by skirting it, showing that it is of later date.

Bronze Age round barrows began large and ended small, with the exception that Beaker barrows are often small. Porton Down is home to the largest barrow in Wiltshire, and it probably has one of the smallest, indeed, a pair of them. The mounds lie on Roche Court Down, close to the Winterslow Hut group, and can be easily overlooked among the long grass. Both are 8m in diameter and 15cm high. Both have been excavated. One is described as a memorial barrow of Anglo-Saxon date; the other contained a Saxon skeleton with an iron knife, a clasp or buckle and a leg of mutton.

Of a particular group of seven barrows lying to the west of the Range four have suffered from past ploughing. One of the remaining, a bell barrow, was excavated during the First World War by Sir Roger Galliway, who recovered what would now be classed as a Middle Bronze Age urn. Others were excavated by William Cunnington.

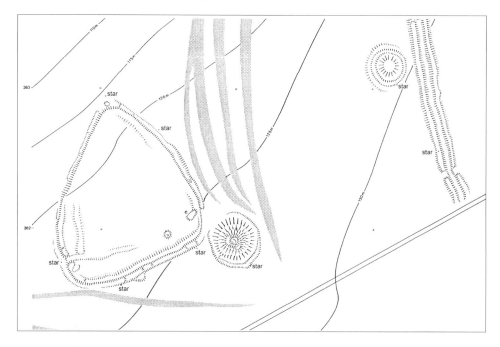

36 RCHME's survey of the D-feature enclosure and round barrow on Idmiston Down. © *Crown Copyright. NMR*

One round barrow on Idmiston Down, near Moll Harris Clump, lies at the apex of an enclosure, known technically as a D-feature (*36* and *colour plate 12*). The manner in which the enclosure and the barrow are closely linked suggests that the earthwork had a ritual function. Only one other such enclosure is known to exist in the country.

The placement of round barrows in the landscape has been considered by Ann and Peter Woodward who suggested that barrows cluster around Stonehenge in two rough rings centred on the henge, one ring lying about 1km out and the second double this distance. This differentiation is tentatively ascribed to differences in levels of status by the Woodwards. No such patterning of placement is discernible at Porton Down.

THE URNFIELD ON EASTON DOWN

Stone noticed that a patch of slightly raised ground at the edge of the flint mines had escaped the attention of rabbits; it proved to be a roughly crescentic deposit of large flint nodules some 18 x 6m and 15cm in height. Its slightly dumbbell appearance suggested at first that it might be a pair of flinty barrows that had merged together over time, but such proved not to be the case (*37*). Among the flint capping were two flint scrapers, a small pointed tool and an implement very similar to the waisted tool

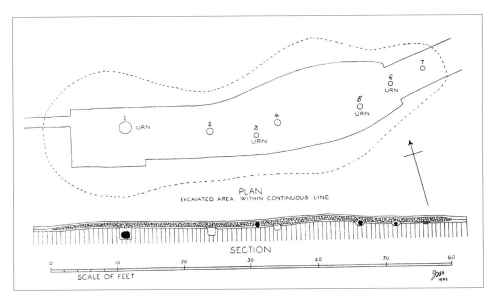

37 Plan of Stone's 'urnfield' cairn on Easton Down. *Courtesy WANHM*

38 The urns from Stone's 'urnfield' on Easton Down. *Courtesy Salisbury Museum*

that Stone thought might have been a plane. Beneath the flint nodules lay several small pits, or cists, which had been cut into the chalk.

The first cist was 50cm in diameter and 45cm deep. Inside lay 90 fragments of a Collared Urn, red in colour and over 30cm in height (*38*). It had been packed around with ashes and contained the cremated bones of a child of eight years of age or so, cleaned of ash. The presence of eight beads, four of jet, three of amber and one of faience (*colour plate 5*), suggested to Stone that the burial was of a girl. It was the faience bead that eventually set Stone on the path that led to his consideration of faience in Egypt and India. There was also a small bone pin or awl. Cist 2 was smaller and held charcoal and the bones of a child of some five years of age, and five pieces of burnt flint. Next in line lay an urn 13cm tall in 74 fragments, badly fired and not interred in a cist. There were no ashes present, and Stone speculated that the urn had been smashed through being dropped. Cist 4 (there was no Cist 3, its place taken by the urn) was 23cm in diameter and 15cm deep. It contained a little charcoal and three small pieces of burnt bone, but no urn. Cist 5 was a shallow, scooped-out hole, on the bottom of which lay a crushed Collared Urn, brown in colour and made of badly fired clay, probably buried in the inverted position; it originally stood just over 13cm in height. Cist 6 was also a scooped out hole, no more than 15cm across, containing 55 shards of a small Collared Urn; there were two small fragments of bone. Cist 7 was simply a hole cut in the chalk containing 'mould and flints'.

Arguing from the forms of the urns, Stone concluded that the urnfield was of Middle Bronze Age construction, 'not much earlier than 1000 BC'. Radiocarbon dating has since shown that the span of prehistory is much larger than formerly imagined, and that Stone's estimate of the date of the urnfield was greatly in error. About 450m east of the urnfield, lies an Early Middle Bronze Age cemetery with remarkable similarities, discovered in 1983 and with two calibrated radiocarbon dates (see below), with no more than 20 years between their central estimates, which average 1725 BC (calibrated). The cultural parallels between the two cemeteries are such that Stone's urnfield may confidently be dated to this approximate date, too.

It is remarkable that the urnfield survived at all. Elsewhere in the area, as we shall discuss, the gunflint knappers of the eighteenth and nineteenth centuries exploited practically every concentrated source of raw material they found. Stone discovered their debitage in a Neolithic shaft, and gunflint cores are scattered throughout the downs. It is inconceivable that the gunflint workers were not aware of the urnfield's potential as raw material, unlikely, too, that they either knew or cared about its funerary aspect. Survival, then, as is often the case, was a matter of unfathomable chance.

A CREMATION CEMETERY AND FLINT CAIRN
OF THE EARLY MIDDLE BRONZE AGE

In 1983, a small flint cairn was discovered, less than 2m in visible diameter and about 15cm high, at an area of the Range known as Blake's Firs (*39*). A small excavation was initiated to determine the composition of the cairn, first placing four trial trenches to the cardinal points to assess the nature of the ground on which it lay, for depressions in the ground extending from the Easton Down mining complex to just south of the cairn indicated a possible link to it. The 'small excavation' lasted until 1993 and was published in 2001 (*40*).

The northerly trial trench cut through two pit cremation burials, each about 50cm in diameter and depth, set into the chalk bedrock, both filled with ash, charcoal, burnt flint, burnt soil and the cremated remains of bones and teeth. It was apparent that the undifferentiated remains of funeral pyres had been deposited in the pits, which had been covered with large, flat flints. There was no indication of disturbance prior to excavation, except that of the ubiquitous rabbit. Fortunately, the ground had never been ploughed. It was clear that a wider excavation than that envisaged originally was desirable. In all, seven pit cremation burials were revealed, arranged in a line passing to the east of the cairn, and a further two burials off the line, both uncharacteristic of the other seven and dissimilar to each other. Some of the pits

39 Blake's Firs Cairn under excavation

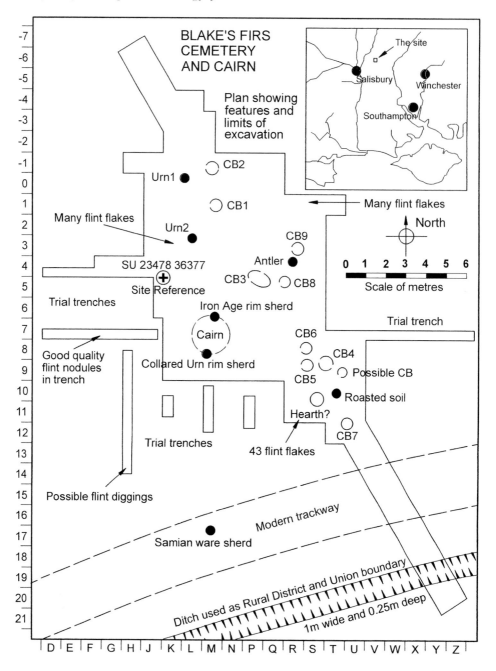

40 Plan of the Bronze Age cremation cemetery and cairn at Blake's Firs

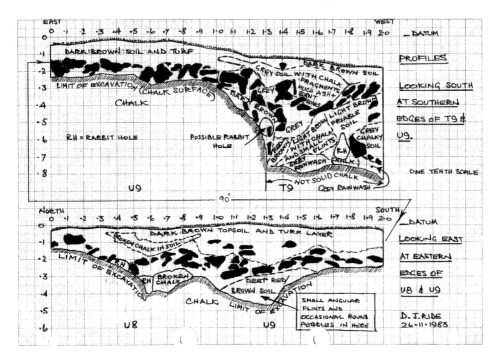

41 A page from the author's excavation notebook showing disturbance by rabbits of a cremation burial at Blake's Firs

had been badly damaged by rodents, but the others were untouched (*41* and *colour plate 8*). Crushed remains from two miniature Collared Urns were discovered to the north of the cairn. Other ceramic remains were recovered, all of them fractured and disturbed by rabbit activity. There were fragments of a single Beaker and unidentified components of coarser vessels, possibly larger urns. A single rim sherd of an Iron Age vessel was found near the edge of the cairn, and one sherd of Roman Samian ware was washed by rain from the track to the south of the cairn, possibly indicating continuing respect for the mound. Numerous worked flints were recovered, but only one identifiable tool, a crude scraper. Large nodules of good quality flint were found 0.4m below the surface in the western trial trench along with possible flint 'diggings', a series of small depressions that cut into the flint seam, that lay within 10m of the cairn, in the south-south-west and north-east directions. However, the ground was very disturbed having attracted the energetic attention of the rabbits, which explains the tentative label of flint 'diggings' here.

The excavation of the cairn consisted of removing one flint at a time; they were of small or moderate size, nodules or tabular flints, such as could be obtained from surface deposits. A few worked flakes were found, but as these were abundant across the site their presence in the cairn was not remarkable. A cross section of the cairn (*42*) shows that it had partially sunk into the chalk over the millennia. Its weight

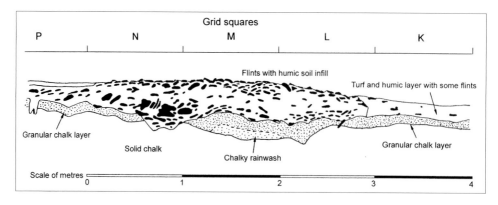

42 A cross section of the cairn at Blake's Firs

and attractiveness to perching birds – with the attendant concentration of uric acid – had combined to fracture and rot the underlying chalk allowing subsidence to occur. Gravity prevailed, and the flint pile had inevitably spread. A number of large tabular flints at the base of the cairn, arranged off-centre, suggested the presence of a collapsed cist. The structure appeared to lie only partially below the original ground surface, as did the cists of Stone's urnfield cairn. No bones, pottery or charcoal were discovered in the postulated cist – a well-defined rabbit burrow ran centrally under the cairn into it, as if directed by radar. Several large flint nodules were discovered in the cairn's north-eastern quadrant, 1.5m from the centre, which may have formed part of a rudimentary kerb to the cairn. The ground beneath the cairn was excavated down to, and into, the undisturbed chalk, but no shafts or burials were found.

The first burial discovered was the most intact of the pits, and was broadly typical of the rest, so it will be described in detail here. It was circular, some 50cm in diameter, and its flat bottom lay 60cm below the ground surface. The pit had a covering of large flint capstones. Within the fill were over 1kg of calcined human bones, evidently the remains of a single individual, rather unevenly cremated. Not all the body parts were represented in the remains, although the presence of finger bones suggests that everything that survived the fire was buried conscientiously. The condition of the skull sutures and the degree of wear on a premolar tooth indicate a mature adult. The small frontal suture and the gracile form of the frame tended to indicate that the individual was female. Charcoal from the pit was dated by radiocarbon analysis to 1950–1500 BC (HAR-5889, calibrated).

The second burial discovered, this time of a small child, was similar to the first, but contained only small amounts of bone. Charcoal from this burial was also dated by radiocarbon analysis to 1940–1490 BC (HAR-6944, calibrated). The next burial was ovoid in shape and relatively shallow, with the cremated bones of an adult at one end and those of a child at the other. The next two pits were largely damaged and emptied by rabbits, but a sherd of a Beaker was found inside one and a few flecks of cremated bone and charcoal in the other. Adjacent to this pit was an area of grey, concreted material, probably the emptied contents of the burial. The next two pits were also casualties of rabbits, but contained a few human remains, and in one a sherd from a Beaker. More sherds from the same vessel were found in the rabbit runs around the pit.

Only one cremation burial yielded grave goods. It did not form part of the linear arrangement and lay in light brown, granular, chalky soil that filled an irregular solution hole in the chalk. The bones were compactly arranged in a perfectly circular bun-shape, indicating that they had been contained originally in a flexible bag, probably of woven fabric or animal skin. They had been cleaned of all ash and charcoal and crushed into small pieces. This was clearly a different burial practice from all the others. The burial included 0.6kg of calcined bones; the larger, flat pieces from the skull lay at the bottom of the deposit. Sutures in the occipital region of the skull were not fully closed, and it was deduced that the bones belonged to an individual aged from 10–12 years, a deduction supported by the presence of two deciduous teeth and the size of the palate, which was nearly complete. (A forensic pathologist undertaking voluntary scrub clearance just happened to be working within hailing distance when the burial was discovered.) The axis bone of the spine was also present, and some finger bones. The deposit clearly represented the remains of only one individual.

Centrally positioned on top of the bones lay a bronze awl 54.5mm long. It was still sharp, and one end was hammered or cast flat as if to fit into a handle. Indeed, 15mm of this tang differed in appearance from the rest of the awl, as if the surface had undergone a chemical reaction with acids in a wooden or bone handle before it had rotted away or been discarded when the awl was used for its last function. It is likely that the awl had been used to pin the bag together, but that is not to say that it served only a utilitarian function in the act of burial. (Recall here the cremated remains found in an urn and wrapped in a cloth fastened with an awl, buried in a flint cairn overlying a barrow only one 1km away in the Winterslow Hut group of barrows.) On top of the awl lay a black shale barrel bead, its hole formed by opposing, acute depressions in the faces, consistent with drilling from both ends using a conical bit, then two circular quoit beads carved from stone or fashioned from ceramic, of different colours. At a distance of 50mm from this pile rested a cylindrical segment of a fossil belemnite (the internal skeleton of an extinct type of cuttlefish commonly found in the Tarrant Chalk), most probably used as a bead (*colour plate 6*). This assemblage, and that from the urnfield on Easton Down, bears striking resemblances to one discovered by Stone in a barrow on Stockbridge Down.

The awl from Blake's Firs was photographed using an electron microscope. Longitudinal wear marks visible near the tip suggested a degree of use, and latitudinal marks on the tang were consistent with it having been faced up on a stone or by a file. An electron probe analysis of the awl showed it to be made from a high tin content copper alloy, with an original estimated contribution of 13 per cent to 14 per cent tin. Such an alloy provides a high level of hardness together with relative ease of working. There were trace impurities of arsenic and sulphur. The proportion of tin, arsenic and sulphur is very similar to that occurring in the dagger from the earlier Bush Barrow burial, and from the awl found in the Stockbridge barrow. The Blake's Firs awl is thus fashioned from typical materials used in the Bronze Age.

About 50cm north of this burial, under the humic soil, lay an arrangement of flints, composed of two tabular pieces encircled by seven nodules. The ovoid ring, measuring 50 x 30cm, included a near spherical pot-boiler. To the north of this structure lay an antler from a red deer, about three years old; the brow and bez tines, having been broken off, were absent. The main tine had been snapped off 160mm from the tip and lay at a sharp angle to the main shaft of the antler, the break lying under the pot-boiler. The appearance of the arrangement suggested a ritually despoiled deposit and a platform, possibly for further deposits or offerings. The antler could have been deposited as an artefact, thus falling into the category of 'grave goods' – perhaps being a tool of the trade for a flint miner, despoiled by deliberate breakage as a mark of irreversible dedication or so that it would not be recovered for use by someone unconcerned with desecration. Alternatively, it could be viewed in a more symbolic manner, as representative of the vital force of an impressive and powerful animal whose energies are pressed into the service of the dead, or sacrificed to a greater spirit by a ritual offering of this nature.

One further cremation burial was discovered lying off the line of the linearly disposed pits, consisting of a mere 0.21kg of calcined bones and a small incisor tooth, most likely from a child. It rested on the natural chalk surface within an irregular ring of five flint nodules, 18cm in diameter and 25cm below the present ground surface. There was no ash or charcoal present, only a pot-boiler lying nearby. Whereas the scale of the other cremations, involving the construction of large pyres necessary for the incineration of adult bodies and the burial of their remains in a consistent manner, points to a communal effort, the mean aspect of this burial displays an act of disposal within the capabilities of an individual.

Samples of charcoal from two of the pits were submitted for identification. One contained oak, field maple and a type of prunus (cherry, bird cherry or blackthorn) while the other's charcoal was predominantly produced from field maple, with traces of ash (*Fraxinus excelsior*) and hazel. Apart from the oak, isolated specimens of which grow locally now, the other woods are common species of the mainly open downland. The variety of wood in the samples, and their differences in composition between samples, suggest the fortuitous gathering of material for the pyre, rather than any ritually significant species being selected.

About 40 per cent of a miniature undecorated bipartite Collared Urn, originally 110mm tall, was discovered in fragments lying on its side on top of the natural chalk surface next to a large and isolated flint nodule, about 5m to the north of

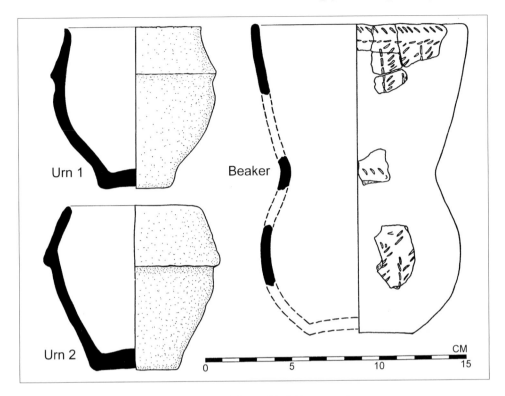

Urn 1

Beaker

Urn 2

CM

0   5   10   15

43 Miniature Collared urns and Beaker vessel from Blake's Firs cremation cemetery

the cairn (*43*). It was fired to a dark red colour outside and black inside (*colour plate 7*). It is closely similar in shape to one of the urns in the urnfield on nearby Easton Down. The remains were lifted in their matrix of soil and excavated on the bench. Only three small, flat, thin fragments of material were discovered; under the microscope they resembled cremated bone.

A second Collared Urn was discovered 3m to the north of the first (*43*). The base lay upright on the surface of the chalk with the body collapsed and broken; one side lying on top of the other, and 70 per cent of the fabric was recovered. It was coarse and almost black, so the fragments were at first mistaken for charcoal. The remains were fragile, probably owing to inadequate firing. No charcoal, bone or other material was discovered with the urn. Attempts to reconstruct the vessel were hampered by its crumbly nature, but it could be determined that it was similar in shape and size to the first urn. It was undecorated and unsymmetrical, as if warped during firing or squashed while green. It was similar to the urn from the urnfield on Easton Down 'made of brownish badly fired clay'. There are further examples of Collared Urns in funerary contexts in the area. M.A. Hamilton, in an unpublished PhD thesis, lists 12 of them from his Salisbury Plain study area of 1995; 11 of them are similar in pattern. Two held only 'token' deposits of bone.

Other similar urns have been found locally at Collingbourne Kingston, Winterslow and Durrington (illustrated in Longworth *Collared Urns of the Bronze Age*, 1984).

Sufficient sherds and fragments of the Beaker were recovered from the rim, waist and body to enable an attempt at its reconstruction (*43*). A line of square impressions, probably executed with a whittled twig or a bird bone ran round the lip, below which was a cord-impressed line. A similar line encircled the waist. The body decoration was of vertical lines of herring-bone pattern, probably incised with a finger nail. The colour of the fabric is typical of late Beakers, and fits most closely Group 5 of the scheme proposed by Lanting and Van der Waals in 1972, in their *Helinium* article 'British beakers as seen from the continent'. Using this classification dates the vessel to 2100–1800 BC, not inconsistent with the radiocarbon dates from the cremation burials, allowing for generalisations in the scheme and tolerances inherent in the radiocarbon assays. (Case, in Kinnes *et al.* 'Radiocarbon dating and British Beakers', 1991, concludes that the most realistic precision that one can hope to attain using radiocarbon dating is currently a span of 250 years.) No obvious parallels, with respect to both shape and decoration of the Beaker, could be found in D.L. Clarke's well-known corpus of beakers of 1970.

One of the 1,320 flint fragments recovered from the site was a core rejuvenation flake. The striking platform of a prismatic core from which long flakes are struck becomes reduced in diameter relative to the core's central dimension, and ragged, because the protruding bulbs of percussion of the detached flakes eat into it. The old striking platform was removed by a transverse blow in an act of rejuvenation. The resulting flake is like a biscuit from which bites have been taken all round. This discovery is more usually associated with Mesolithic or Early Neolithic techniques and suggests that advanced knapping occurred on the site before the cemetery was placed there, consistent with the widespread and indiscriminately occurring scatter of the bulk of the debitage recovered. However, this was not the case with a collection of 43 small flint flakes, two of which fitted together – so confirming their status as an assemblage – which were recovered from an area about 60cm square located 3m from the cairn's edge. They were tentatively ascribed to the Middle Bronze Age from their shape. They would not have survived as a group owing to the intense activity on the site had they predated the cemetery. This assemblage recalls the discovery of a knapping event on a barrow-like feature near the Breck area of the Porton Down Range. In addition to its utilitarian function, knapping an implement at a ritual site, or simply creating flakes, may have possessed a measure of significance for some ancient people. Julian Richards in his book *Stonehenge* describes 'a tightly-defined cluster of flint flakes and cores' discovered in the ditch of the Stonehenge Cursus, 'the result of perhaps only a few minutes of knapping'. The question is posed for us, but is not yet answerable, of whether or not people with a strong sense of location felt compelled to perform a skilled and individual act productive of a residue in a ritual of commemoration or propitiation. Some parallel is discernable in the modern practice of leaving flowers at the site of a fatal road accident.

Marcus Stone described the Stockbridge Down cairn as a barrow, and while this terminology is technically correct it may be more appropriate and fruitful to recognise, at least locally, the class of monuments identified by flint cairn burials, for other examples exist. Stone records in his second excavation notebook a cairn on the Porton Down Range lying 1.2km north of Blake's Firs:

> … twenty-five feet in diameter and nine inches high composed almost entirely of flints, forming a cairn which appears to have settled down and spread … A small scooped-out hole, very irregular, was found almost central … about twelve inches in diameter … Fragments of a completely crushed urn of overhanging rim type [Collared Urn] were unearthed … but hardly any ashes were found.

He records another, 3.7km south-west of Blake's Firs, 5.5m in diameter and 25cm high, with 145 'intentionally deposited flint flakes and a core' and a central cist full of charcoal and the cremated bones of an adult. The ground around the cairns was not examined. The similarities of both monuments to features of the Blake's Firs complex are marked, but the greatest parallels lie with the Stockbridge Down burial. The quoit beads and shale beads are practically identical to the Blake's Firs bag burial, and both contained a bronze awl of similar pattern and composition.

The main feature of the Blake's Firs cemetery is the arrangement in line of the similar pit cremations, an approximate linear grouping echoed by Stone's urnfield. He gives a further example from Lancaster Moor where urns had been placed in pairs 'at intervals of a yard in a long line extending east and west'. Barrett, reporting on Bronze Age cremation cemeteries from Middlesex in 1973, also describes an instance of multiple rows of linearly placed urns, at Ashford Common, Sunbury. There is also the local example of an accurate alignment of nine round barrows of the Bronze Age to the axis of a long barrow at Winterbourne Stoke, 2km west of Stonehenge; a similar arrangement of barrows is visible at nearby Normanton Down. All or some of the burials considered may have resulted from a prescribed ritual procedure involving alignment, but the practice may have arisen to denote the temporal sequence of the deposits to ensure the correct identification of those buried rather than as an aspect of ritual importance. In the case of the flat cremation cemetery it also helps guard against the disturbance of previous burials, supposing that the previous burial, although flat, is still visible or marked in some way. Coles and Harding, in their *Bronze Age in Europe* of 1979, interpret multiple row burials as family groupings, and it is reasonable to include in this view single family cemeteries where only one row is present.

There is a rich density of such sites on the Porton Down Range and nearby, displaying a common ritual package that includes cremation burials both in urns and directly in pits; the construction of flint cairns; the use of Beakers and, later, miniature Collared Urns; the deposition of beads of various composition; and the employment of bronze awls, sometimes with a 'fastening' function. Not all elements occur at every site, of course. The major question regarding funerary practices of the time is why there should be disposal of bodies both by inhumation and cremation, but here is not the place to review the matter. However, we may note without controversy that inhumation often involved a greater deployment of effort with the raising of large earthen barrows over the dead; that cremation burials frequently occur at earlier inhumation sites; and that Beakers are notably associated with inhumations (the classic 'crouched beaker burials' for example) and have been discovered with grave goods of gold.

When one looks at the great wealth deposited in some burials it is not unreasonable to conclude that a marked hierarchical division existed in Bronze Age society, although the extent of migration of ideas, traditions and personnel across the 'class' boundary can be only roughly assessed. It is easy to envisage a dominant society practising inhumation allowing the cremation burial of social inferiors to occur within the precincts of its graves, for acknowledgement and acceptance of subservient behaviour is implied and a perception of centrality established. It is harder to imagine such an aristocracy ignoring the insertion of the cremated remains of others in its grandest monuments unless their authority had passed away. However, this model may be clouded by regionally dependent chronological differences in burial practices.

Avoiding this controversial territory, let us examine critically the differences among the individual graves at Blake's Firs. The putative cist within the cairn suggests that it was a grave, and the monumental aspect of the cairn formed the focus for the further burials, seven of which strongly conformed to a common pattern. Jacqueline McKinley, discussing the connection between barrows and rites of cremation in a *Proceedings of the Prehistoric Society* paper of 1997, notes that cremations may also have included combustible pyre goods. Richly provided funerals may thus have left residues indistinguishable from poor ones. Burial is but one process in the funeral rite, its importance relative to other components not necessarily remaining constant. Residues may not be diagnostic of the overall level of funerary resources expended, which may be a more critical indicator of wealth or social standing. High-status remains may sometimes receive only superficial, token burial, if any, the bulk being retained for other ritual purposes conducted away from the burial site, the level of retention perhaps related directly to the degree of status.

The treatment of the remains of the burial with grave goods may mark a distinction of sex, class or occupation rather than a departure from existing group ritual or a demonstration of economic superiority. Moore and Rowlands, in their *Bronze Age metalwork in Salisbury Museum*, cite the discovery of a similar awl in a cremation burial within an inverted urn at the centre of a barrow 8.5km to the north-west, near Amesbury. They postulate that this type of awl is typical of female graves in the

Wessex Culture, the presumed dominant society at this time. (Views regarding the Wessex Culture are changing with the discovery of other contemporary rich burials outside Wessex.) Some awls may have been manufactured from bronze specifically as metal grave goods or identified as a small, and thus relatively cheap item of domestic origin, when a deposit of bronze was called for by custom.

Although somewhat distant, the similarities in other European cultural practices allow us to consider the evidence from a near-contemporary cemetery in Hungary, given by Chapman and Randsborg in *The archaeology of death*, 1974, that beads were confined to female burials, but it is unclear whether they, like Stone, assessed a grave as female by the presence of beads. It is noteworthy that assemblages of beads contain a variety of patterns. Stone's urnfield beads were of amber, shale, ceramic (or stone) and faience. All the beads from Blake's Firs differ from one another in pattern, size or material, and occur in a burial proved as female from forensic evidence. It is clear that here the beads and awl are not simply a sentimental deposit of the randomly garnered effects of the deceased; rather, they are drawn from an orthodox catalogue of prescribed goods. Undoubtedly, these grave goods possessed ritual meaning, but perhaps not until bestowed at burial; until then they may have served as ornaments, or held utilitarian or trading value.

Within Blake's Firs cemetery, the unique nature of this burial in its possession of undisputed artefactual grave goods accords with the observation by Ann Ellison that where such artefacts occur they are distributed one per site or cluster. This may account for the presence and nature of the burial, rather than social differentiation. The presence of a single more richly endowed, and more carefully treated, female burial, differentiated topographically from the more robustly performed burials, may be anticipated from the statement by Richard Bradley that:

> There is evidence for the burial of whole families or communities rather than that of one part of society; there is evidence that women may have enjoyed roughly the same status as men.

More than this, the positive identification of a rich female burial presents the possibility that only women or girls qualified for the 'one per site' provision. Determination of the matter would provide further insights into Bronze Age society.

Ellison records that 52 per cent of Middle Bronze Age cemeteries contain fewer than 12 burials, most commonly between 10 and 25, 'situated within or beside a barrow, or, occasionally, forming a small, flat cemetery'. Positioned within these criteria, and with each possessing a single child burial with grave goods, of which one was definitely female, the two cemeteries on Easton Down may be considered similar and typical of the age.

As noted, some dead were not simply disposed of: they became a resource, collectively, individually or as body parts. The barrow situated to the west of Blake's Firs where only a skull was buried is an example of the use of a body part. Cemeteries are archives of the ancestors; they provide sanctification of, and authority for, possession of the land they occupy. Where they border other graves, they proclaim that the territories they define possess title. The problem lies with the area between such cemeteries. Most current border disputes are between neighbours fighting for control of a few centimetres of fence land. Close to the cairn at Blake's Firs, and south of it, runs a shallow ditch thought to be of Late Bronze Age date aligned north-east to south-west, used in modern times as a Rural District and Union boundary. It was sectioned by the Blake's Firs excavation but yielded no dating evidence. This could be a case where land division was defined with regard to ancient title by running the ditch between the two cemeteries.

However, there could be more dominant pressures on the placement of burial sites, such as the visibility of distant monuments or the occupation of ridge crests and hilltops. But just as round barrows cluster around Stonehenge, the Blake's Firs cremation burials seem consciously to seek to share the location of the cairn. It is to this monument that placement criteria should perhaps apply, the most plausible of which is its situation on a false crest so that it would have appeared as a skyline feature when viewed from lower down the slope looking north. It is considered that false cresting dictates the direction from which the monument should be viewed or approached. Of all the barrows on the Porton Down Range there is only one other, on the ridge of Idmiston Down, that lies on a false crest.

THE SETTLEMENTS ON EASTON DOWN

Marcus Stone identified the settlements adjacent to the area of Neolithic flint mines from scatters of surface finds consisting of sherds of Beaker vessels and allied pottery, burnt flints and animal bones in an area that had been all but levelled by cultivation. He acknowledged in his excavation report that 'no direct association [had] yet been observed' between the mines and the settlements, but over time came to connect the two. Lacking a sound chronology, he was justified in his opinion to an extent, at least in reasonable speculation. The settlements encircled the main area of flint mines and, although much later than them, their inhabitants may have also extracted flint from there. His assessment of a connection was no doubt affected by the discovery of Neolithic material in the settlements, but the proximity of the mines could account for their presence. He excavated two pits in Area A, the first of which was 3m long by 1.2m wide. The undisturbed habitation layer was encountered at a depth of between 15cm and 30cm, varying in thickness from 15-25cm. Within it were bones and teeth from oxen and sheep, fragments from

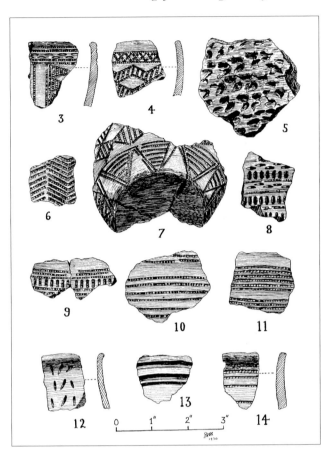

44 Pottery from Pit A2 at Easton Down. *Courtesy WANHM*

5 Beakers and 4 other vessels (*44*), a burnt flint arrowhead, 14 thumbnail scrapers, 5 core scrapers, an end scraper, 12 knives and 6 slender flakes. Stone found five stake holes on the pit's north-eastern side, and he postulated that rabbits had destroyed more on the other sides. Giving weight to this postulation, Stone wrote: 'These stake holes undoubtedly indicate an above-ground wooden structure.' The second excavated pit resembled the first, containing a few pieces of bone, plain pottery and burnt flint. Stone then excavated a pit 3.4m in diameter and 90cm deep from Area B, placing a trial trench across it. This also contained fragments of pottery, flint flakes, burnt flint and a hammerstone.

An area 15m square was uncovered 200m west of this last pit, revealing evidence of 10 circular and oval depressions and shallow holes (*45*). Stone identified them as temporary shelters rather than permanent homes. There were no stratified habitation layers and a paucity of refuse; none of the pits contained a hearth. Fragments of Beaker pottery, worked flint and bone were found. One 'hut' contained an ash pit, 70cm in diameter and of similar depth; with the ash occupying the lower 25cm. On analysis it was found to contain fine chalk dust, minute particles of wood and what

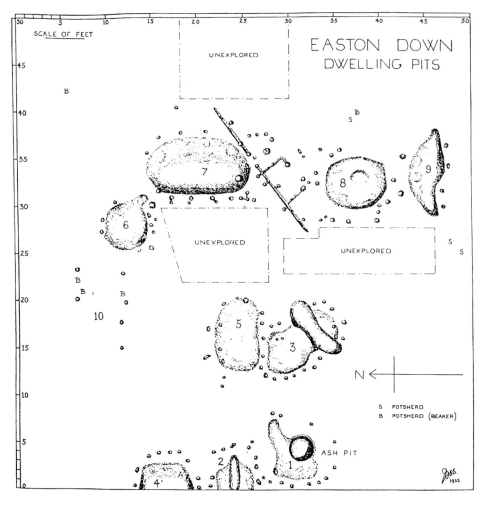

45 Stone's 'dwelling pits' on Easton Down. *Courtesy WANHM*

could have been bone ash, suggested by a high percentage of calcium phosphate (Stone was a chemist, remember), but no charcoal. With it were distributed small pieces of bone from oxen and pigs, flint flakes and fragments of reddish pottery. No definite conclusion was reached on what the pit was used for or what utility its contents might have held for its owners. Two more ash pits were subsequently discovered, not within any putative habitation structure but with stake holes nearby, suggestive of them being fenced or walled. The complete skeleton of a dog, of fox terrier type, was recovered from the base of one, 'lying in an attitude of sleep with head on front paws and hind legs curled up with the tail between them' (*46*). Was the inclusion of the animal a factor in the cultural lexicon of the pits, or was the animal so highly regarded that it was deliberately covered in the 'seemingly precious ashes'? Stone could not tell.

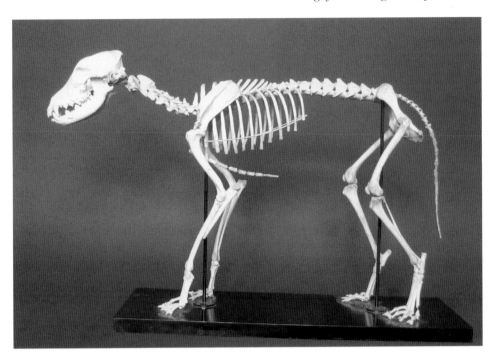

46 Prehistoric dog's skeleton from Easton Down. *Courtesy Salisbury Museum*

All the pits were surrounded by stake holes. Between huts seven and eight there lay a straight furrow 5m long. Offset to either side were rows of stake holes. This structure Stone interpreted as the supported wattle side of a Neolithic house, the remains of which had been built over, or as a screen between the two 'huts'. He favoured the latter explanation because sherds of Neolithic pottery were found in these and one other 'hut', but none elsewhere, except in a pit in Area B. He wrote concerning the forms of pottery in the 'huts': 'We are thus forced to the conclusion that cultural borrowing has taken place, presumably from Windmill Hill to the Peterborough [culture].' Stone reinforced his conclusion by including in his report plans of Neolithic houses from Goldberg, Germany. However, the wedge-shaped cross sections of the pits in Area A present unlikely house profiles, and there are problems with the stratigraphy. The lower layers of the pit were described by Stone as 'sterile rainwash' and the 'habitation' material appears very much a secondary event. In Area B, the irregularly shaped 'dwelling' might be the result of other human activities, or even tree throws. It is by no means clear that a connection necessarily exists between the stake holes and the pits. One putative hut site differs very little from the shallow mine shafts at Easton Down.

Of the flint implements, Stone chose to illustrate five, considering them of particular significance. One he described as a 'sharply-waisted, steep-sided, massive scraper of plane' with a flat, unflaked undersurface. The tool is very similar to the one described above from the Tower Hill excavation, except for the latter's notched cutting or scraping edge. This notch may have been an accident of knapping, and the reason why it was discovered, perhaps discarded, near the Tower Hill knapping area. Such may have been the reason for the recovery of the ficron from the worked area at Martin's Clump for, although its workmanship is of a high standard, one face is disfigured by a large, unsightly flake scar.

The nature of the relationship between the flint mines and the other traces of human activity on the site still remains unclear and readily open to alternative interpretations. The radiocarbon date on the one hand and the pottery on the other indicate a time span of over 1,000 years. A rectangular enclosure south of the mines appears to be incorporated into Celtic fields that exist there, but the chronological relationship between them has been destroyed by ploughing. Celtic fields are dated to the Middle or Late Bronze Age, but rectangular enclosures also occur alongside the Neolithic flint mines at Cissbury, Blackpatch and Harrow Hill. Fortunately, the Easton Down site possesses great excavation potential, so the issue may be capable of resolution.

THE THORNEY DOWN FARMSTEAD

The importance of Marcus Stone's discovery of the Thorney Down farmstead to the understanding of such features, and those who populated them, is widely acknowledged. His search for the farm was prompted by his previous examination of the enclosure on Boscombe Down East, which he interpreted as a corral, and his identification of those linear features running towards the River Bourne as ranch boundaries. He always sought to interpret his findings as a unified narrative and his story would be incomplete without the crofts and tofts of the farmers.

The excavation proceeded in two phases. Four sections were placed across a short stretch of ditch lying to the north of the site; its eastern terminal was also excavated. The finds consisted of many pot-boilers, flint flakes, scrapers, a flint knife, a few potsherds and the lumbar bones of a small ox. An area 10 x 11m was then stripped of turf, revealing 33 clearly defined post-holes, with no well-defined pattern. More than 1,000 pot-boilers were recovered and some 600 sherds of pottery, similar to that found from the enclosure on Boscombe Down East, dateable to the Late Bronze Age. One object of bronze was recovered as six small fragments, near a post-hole. On reconstruction this turned out to be a small section of a bracelet, a cast object, embellished with tooling, with five circumferential ribs (47), similar to one found at West Buckland, in Somerset, associated with a double-looped palstave (a bronze axe without sockets) and another – also with five ribs – in the Edlington Bronze hoard in the same county.

The second phase of the investigation extended the excavated area to 34 x 26m. More post-holes were found, and the usual minor finds. There were enough sherds

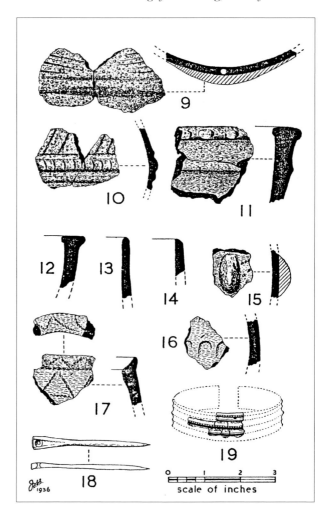

47 Pottery, bone needle and bronze bracelet from the Thorney Down farmstead. *Courtesy WANHM*

from one domestic vessel to reconstruct it (*48*). It measured 140mm tall and 180mm in diameter and was identified as a domestic vessel of the Late Bronze Age. When Stone discovered a double-looped spearhead 106mm long on the site he took it home, placed it on a page in his notebook and drew round it with his pen (*49*).

Ann Ellison's re-examination of Stone's 'remarkable excavations' began as an analysis of the functional characteristics of Middle Bronze Age pottery assemblages; but she discovered his detailed site records in Salisbury Museum and was furnished with a copy of his recently discovered second excavation notebook. She bravely undertook the tasks of determining the chronological development of the settlement, the reconstruction of the plans of individual buildings, and the distribution of the artefacts among the various structures and spaces within the settlement (*50*). Ellison noted that some of the finds and features relate to pre-Deverel-Rimbury phases of activity, and identified structures overlaid by others, and a complex of cooking holes.

48 Late Bronze
Age domestic vessel
from the Thorney
Down farmstead.
*Courtesy H.M.
Darlow*

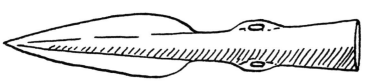

49 Bronze spear
head from Thorney
Down farmstead
as illustrated by
Marcus Stone in
his excavation
notebook. *Courtesy
H.M. Darlow*

These features she ascribed to the Early Bronze or Early Middle Bronze Ages; other structures she related to one or more phases of Middle Bronze Age occupation. Two huts possess south-easterly facing porches, a feature found in many later Bronze Age and Iron Age sites. Two main phases of development were recognisable. Of 10 large holes recorded by Stone, five are identified tentatively as storage pits, and three – from the presence of ash, charcoal and fire-cracked flint – as hearths. As the site was undisturbed prior to excavation, the distributions and types of artefacts could be related to differentiated activities occurring there. Of the artefacts found, the objects and sherds lacking decorative motifs relate to the early structures: those with strong, moderate and weak patterning correlate with the different categories of structure identified by Ellison. Strong patterning relates to the double-ring houses, which functioned as living quarters, with separate areas for food consumption, tool manufacture and possibly textile production. Moderate patterning occurred in small buildings where food storage, preparation and cooking might have been undertaken. Weakly patterned artefacts are associated with four-post structures, postulated as storage buildings. This arrangement fits the model of a residential house, an ancillary hut, storage facilities, and open-air activity areas, as suggested by a series of Middle Bronze Age sites in southern England, for example at Itford Hill and Black Patch in Sussex.

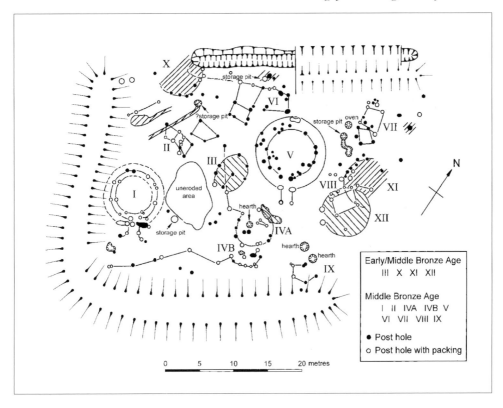

50 Ann Ellison's interpretation of the post-holes of the Thorney Down farmstead. *Redrawn after Ann Ellison with permission*

The Thorney Down settlement was also studied, in a *Proceedings of the Prehistoric Society* paper of 1999, by Joanna Brück, who sought to account for its two-phase nature by postulating models of demographic, social and economic patterning, and relating ritual depositions in such farmsteads to postulated contemporary beliefs in a correspondence between the buildings and their occupants. Brück warned against attempting to fit a standard model to all farmsteads, but by emphasising a lack of generality she weakens the case for some of her own suggestions.

It was only through Marcus Stone's meticulous recording and reporting of his excavations that these valuable assessments of Bronze Age domestic arrangements and beliefs could be explored, using modern ideas and an accumulation of later data. It is only latterly, too, that it has become acceptable to seek answers to outstanding questions by appeals to other cultures that possess similarities and about which more is known.

6

Lines of contention: division of land in the Bronze and Iron Ages

Coastlines, rivers and mountain ranges impose natural boundaries within which nations, tribes and families can exercise control, ownership and the exploitation of land resources. However, this hierarchy of social structures demands a parallel subdivision of the landscape into progressively smaller units of responsibility. As a consequence, the archaeological record contains man-made boundaries with a spectrum of dimensions.

At the lower end of the scale are individual houses and settlements, like those at Thorney Down, and the enclosure at Boscombe Down East, which may have performed the Bronze Age equivalent function of the post-medieval field barn.

The next scale up yields field boundaries. Groups of small, rectangular plots, known as 'Celtic fields', are visible in the ploughsoil at three locations on the Porton Down Range: west of the Pheasant Hotel, part of a large, visible complex stretching south-westwards towards Winterslow; near Lopcombe Corner (*51*); and straddling the railway south of the Hampshire Gap. Nowhere on the Range do they form upstanding monuments, but they are visible as low banks at Cockey Down, to the north-east of Salisbury. Patches of them, some extensive, are scattered about the area, with strongly defined groups to the east and north-east of Danebury Hill. Undoubtedly, many have been destroyed by recent agriculture, and many more would be revealed by marks in the soil were the downland ploughed up.

Largest in the hierarchy are the linear banks and ditches, of which the Porton Down Range contains many kilometres, including a section of one over 10km in length that spans the Range, known as the Quarley High Linear (*52*). Others are shorter, and most likely represent the boundaries of 'ranches'. Some are recognised as trackways. The interpretation of linear features relies on their shapes (their profiles in section), their disposition in the topographical landscape, and their relationships with each other and with other earlier or contemporary archaeological components

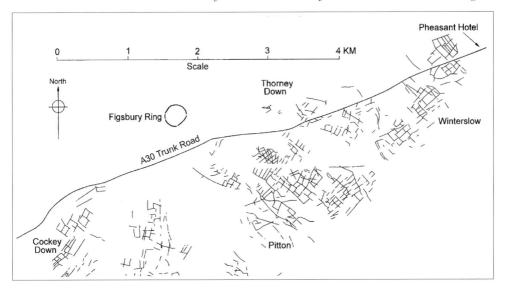

51 Celtic fields on and south of the Porton Down Range. Linear features are not shown. *Adapted and redrawn from R. Palmer (RCHME)*

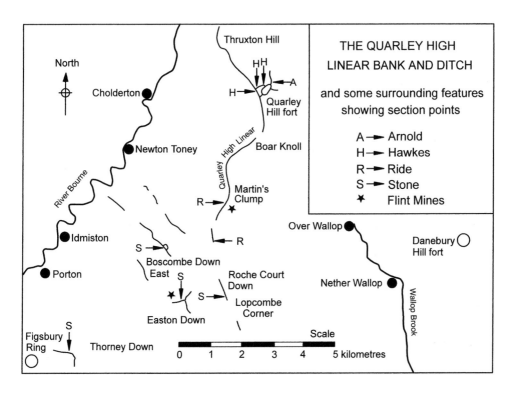

52 Plan of the Quarley High Linear earthwork and other local linear features

of the land. Some linear features form boundaries to Celtic fields and so are judged to predate them or form contemporaneous features; others cut across the fields, demonstrating their later date. Current archaeological thinking regards them generally and collectively as a 'system'. Some were laid out in the Late Bronze Age but most seem to be of Iron Age construction.

Set within the scatter of settlements, the clumps of fields and the network of linear features, are the Iron Age hill-forts, circular earthworks whose group name conceals the range of purposes for which they were originally constructed or subsequently adapted. At Porton Down, the Iron Age landscape is circumferentially dominated by Figsbury Ring to the south-west, Danebury hill-fort to the east, and Quarley hill-fort immediately to the north (53). Farther afield, a hill-fort was discovered in advance of building works at Boscombe Down West, towards Amesbury, and to the south-west lies Old Sarum, its prehistoric origins concealed by immense Norman earthworks.

Although characteristically an Iron Age phenomenon, some hill-forts were developments of earlier hill-top enclosures. A surge of hill-fort building occurred in the 150 years or so from about 550 BC. Changes in pottery styles also occurred then, and the new patterns exhibit regionally restricted distributions. These phenomena suggest strongly a change in social organisation, a move to smaller, more locally controlled groupings with a need for their own boundaries and secure enclosures. Professor Barry Cunliffe has listed the possible uses for which hill-forts were

53 An aerial view of Quarley hill-fort. © *English Heritage. NMR*

constructed or developed: a social locus within defined territory; a centre for ritual activity; a focus for exchange; and a defended position offering protection when need arose. Individual hill-forts may have performed several of these functions.

In this chapter, I shall examine the relationships among the Celtic fields, the linear features and the hill-forts, studying not just their archaeology but the history of the archaeological thought that has led to their current understanding and the terminology employed in their study. I shall also discuss aspects of archaeology at Porton Down that need reconciliation with the current model of linear features.

CELTIC FIELDS

The most comprehensive analysis of Celtic fields is H.C. Bowen's *Ancient fields*. The rectangular or sub-rectangular fields are typically 0.1-0.6 hectares in area and vary from roughly square to being six times longer than they are broad. Long fields are more suited to tilling with the plough. While most conform to a rough grid pattern, there is a general irregularity not wholly accounted for by the contours of the ground, indicative of piecemeal developments but not haphazard ones. South-facing slopes are no more favoured than north-facing ones, suggesting full land utilisation.

Bowen considers that the boundaries may have been marked out originally by small banks and ditches, or by low banks formed by 'scraping up' and subsequently 'sharpened' on either side by ploughing along a slope, when soil is displaced downhill, a process known as lynchet formation. Deliberate lynchet formation appears to have been practised at times to create terraces. However, the preservation of the pattern of fields suggests that, in general, field boundaries did not 'wander' as a result of lynchet formation. Some fields are bordered by piles of flints, presumably removed from the field to aid cultivation.

It is generally agreed that Celtic fields were laid out by the Middle Bronze Age, say from 1400-1300 BC onwards, and that their construction marked a period of settled social organisation. Some were abandoned, then some of these reclaimed. Evidence exists for their cultivation up to Roman times, at least. Some field patterns today are thought to follow Celtic field boundaries.

THE RING OF HILL-FORTS

Figsbury Ring

Of the three hill-forts surrounding Porton Down, Figsbury Ring was the earliest to have been excavated, by Maud Cunnington in 1924. It is a single-banked enclosure with an internal causewayed ditch and two simple entrances lacking any sign of defensive structure or refinement. The outer ditch is not continuous, being a series of quarries from which the bank material was obtained, which arrangement is also not indicative of a defensive plan. Cunnington found very little evidence of habitation, which prompted her to conclude that it was used on a casual basis only. The structure could have been a ritual one, a suggestion supported by the ploughing up, from the interior of Figsbury Ring in 1704, of a magnificent bronze sword 60cm in length, of a type known as Ewart Park, dating it to 1000–750 BC (*colour plate 14*). Such a valuable object was unlikely to have been lost on open ground and is perhaps best seen as a deliberate ritual deposit within a ritual setting.

Quarley hill-fort

Linear features converging on Quarley hill-fort, and its ramparts, were examined in 1938 by Professor Christopher Hawkes who cut trenches through them. The results were published in a lengthy report in the *Proceedings of the Hampshire Field Club* the following year. He showed that the hill-fort was preceded by a palisaded structure and that the subsequent earthen ramparts covered linear features at its western end, confirming its later date. (A similar radial disposition of linear features to that at Quarley Hill occurs at Sidbury hill-fort which lies 9.5km to the north-north-west.) Quarley was abandoned before being completed. Stuart Piggott suggested to Hawkes that the building of the hill-fort was a response to some scare in the middle phase of the Iron Age 'to which a great deal of such activity should be ascribed in the south of Britain generally'. He makes the comparison with Woodbury, south of Salisbury, where the defensive earthworks were not completed either. Hawkes quotes Dr Bersu, the excavator of Woodbury:

> … folk living in the district were impelled by some threat, the nature of which is as yet unknown to defend their open settlements in level country by banks and ditches … At the same time they began to build very strongly-planned defences in high places better protected by nature – hill-forts which in part were certainly not completed or occupied – suggests that we have here to deal with an event of far-reaching importance.

Hawkes noted that pottery from Quarley hill-fort resembles that from Figsbury Ring and Woodbury. He assessed Quarley's purpose as 'a hill-top refuge for its makers and their flocks and herds in time of emergency only'. From the occupation layers at Quarley, Hawkes concluded that here was 'a small colony of people living in squalor amid their own kitchen refuse', probably the builders of the ramparts. However, the description matches in unpleasantness that of the mess found in Roman garrison rooms in forts on Hadrian's Wall.

The Quarley High Linear (Hawkes's Ditch 1) does not converge with the others, passing 165m to the south-west of the hill-fort, being joined to it by a ditch (Ditch 4) lying at a right-angle to it. Hawkes interpreted Ditch 4 as a palisade ditch which also predated the hill-fort and was truncated by it. He argued that it was the latest ditch and that Ditch 1 was constructed in the Late Bronze Age. Hawkes writes of Quarley Hill: '… few [prominences] of the same natural elevation can command such wide uninterrupted views in all directions.' This is certainly the case but should not be taken, on its own, as evidence for any special function for the hill-fort, for wide views are obtained from most hilltops in the area.

In his report, Hawkes acknowledges Dr J.F.S. Stone as giving him 'indispensable help', and it is apparent that Stone's ideas on his own excavations of linear features influenced him and, as will become apparent, resonated for many decades.

Danebury hill-fort

Danebury (*colour plate 15*) is the most thoroughly researched of the hill-forts, over 57 per cent of its interior having been excavated by Professor Cunliffe during the course of 20 seasons from 1969, and the artefacts discovered within it subjected to analysis by more than 40 specialists. There are three rings of ramparts, the inner one being the earliest, probably constructed in the sixth century BC, enclosing about 5 hectares (12 acres). The second phase entailed the construction of a second rampart to which was added a wooden gate, which was burned down. Then, around 400 BC, the third rampart was constructed, and another gate added, which was also burned. Maintenance of the earthwork continued until about 100 BC, when it was abandoned, as many other hill-forts were at that time.

The interior of the fort was inhabited by an estimated population of 300, living in 50 or more round houses clustered behind the ramparts and along a road through the interior. In the centre were located three, possibly four, shrines. The predominance of sheep bones in the Danebury hill-fort faunal record suggests a well-developed sheep economy, but whether this was based on wool or mutton, or evolved into a nutrient engine for fertilising arable lands, as discussed in the next chapter, is not clear. The part excavation of the huge East Chisenbury midden, discovered near Upavon and dated to 750–600 BC, revealed great numbers of sheep bones and much dung, confirming the importance of sheep to the economy. Cunliffe estimates that the interior of Danebury hill-fort contained over 5,000 grain storage pits, and speculates that the massive capacity of these facilities, and the exercise of ritual there, were responsible for Danebury's regional influence which, on any reasonable assessment involving proximity and land forms, would have included what is now the Porton Down Range.

There is no evidence that the fort itself was the home of the regional elite who may have occupied homesteads outside the ramparts but, for the purpose of exercising control, it would have been unwise for them to have lived far distant. Hierarchical societies are vulnerable to internal rebellion. One school of thought regards the hill-forts as purely ritual monuments, built for purposes of prestige, to impress. While such elements may well have formed part of the contemporary social cultural package, there is the evidence of burned gateways, which was a technique described as practiced by the Gauls and Belgae by Julius Caesar, to suggest one or more episodes of siege. Also, a purely symbolic defence surely would not have strategically placed 11,000 sling stones, gathered from afar, as ammunition to defend the entrance. The first-century Greek historian Diodorus Siculus described the weapons and military equipment of Celtic warriors, every item of which was recovered from Danebury (the possible exception being chariot fittings, which may equally have belonged to carts). Cunliffe is unequivocal about the matter:

> The ramparts, ditches and gates of Danebury, whatever their significance as a means of displaying the prestige of the occupants, were primarily defensive in character.

He writes more generally:

> Taking, then, a broad view of the Middle Iron Age in Britain, there are cogent reasons to argue that in the centre-south endemic warfare, resulting in sporadic raids, was an ever-present reality ....

This view is in line with the writings of another first-century Greek historian Strabo of Amasya, who described the Celts as war mad and quick to battle but, until the arrival of the Romans, had no-one else to fight but themselves. There was no reason for Strabo to slant this description politically, and most historians accept it at face value. The picture of violent behaviour that emerges from the classical writers includes one of formalised conflict, in the nature of a medieval joust, which both defuses aggression while at the same time maintaining military effectiveness and preparedness against any external assault. Certainly, the Celts were known as brave and dangerous warriors, if possessing a penchant for individual action rather than maintaining discipline when attacking. This model of society allows for mutually beneficial activities to occur, such as uninterrupted agriculture and cross-Channel trade. It is, though, inherently unstable, prone to conflicts in earnest, which could be ignited by such low-level aggression as raids for cattle or slaves, or disputes over territory. During such periods, the Avon and other rivers ceased to be lines of contact and commerce and became borders to watch and defend. A good historical parallel is the Rhine in modern times.

Topographically, with this model of society, we should observe the development of a landscape with clear tribal and sub-tribal boundaries, the smaller domains possessing one or more main strong points for refuge – or comforting assurance of refuge – and safe custody of essential supplies and riches. This conforms to the Iron Age Danebury landscape. To the west lies the River Bourne, and beyond that the more substantial barrier of the River Avon. To the east it enjoyed the security provided by the River Test, together with its tributary the River Anton and the Pillhill Brook, a tributary of the Anton. The Wallop Brook provided a measure of defence to the south and east. While fordable, the minor watercourses would have made demands on the energy of any raiders and slowed them down, perhaps providing obstacles more important for impeding the movement of rustled cattle or protesting potential slaves. The hill-fort of Bury Hill to the north of Danebury, overlooking the River Anton on a great spur of chalk, is conveniently sited to provide early warning, at least, of any aggressors converging on Danebury from the north-west. This scenario has room for a garrison outpost at Quarley Hill, and its characteristics fit it for such a conjectured role. That it was not completed probably indicates that the nature of the threat lessened, maybe in response to a general lowering of hostility in society or the removal of a specific, local threat. Alternatively, the western boundary of the Danebury enclave was pushed westwards.

Cunliffe, in *Iron Age Britain*, provides territorial maps based on pottery type distributions. The map for the fourth to second century BC corresponds loosely to the assumed boundaries between the named tribes known by the Romans from the first century BC. This suggests that Danebury's territory ran parallel to the River Avon on its eastern bank, and along the River Bourne, and that it lies at the western boundary of the land later recorded as belonging to the tribe of the Atrebates. Some time in the fourth to second centuries Danebury appears to have been not just a sub-tribal unit but a tribal frontier territory. However, by the first century BC, on the evidence of the pottery, this tribal boundary had been extended north-westwards or, at least, trade/exchange established in this direction. In either case, defended boundaries became unnecessary.

LINEAR BANKS AND DITCHES

There is no dispute that linear features are, in general, the relics of ancient land divisions, with the implication that they also controlled the grazing of stock. A few have been identified as trackways or cattle droves, but the rest, from their length and configuration, are usually termed 'ranch boundaries', forming units larger than Celtic fields. They are almost universally spoken of as the 'Wessex Linear Bank and Ditch System', which is seen as a progressive ordering of the land, a generalisation – *the* system. This masks the fact that linear features were constructed for a variety of purposes and that some, their usefulness having passed, were then employed for other functions, such as raised tracks or new boundaries. Within the 'system', a class of banks and ditches that run for considerable distances, keeping mostly to the high ground, are often termed 'spinal linears' (Hawkes quaintly called them 'travelling ditches'). The Quarley High Linear falls into this category. Here, it will be necessary to examine the 'spinal linear' model in respect of this feature.

Marcus Stone's interpretation of a sunken way bordered by post-holes lying near Ford is a reasonable one, possibly the only reasonable one; but Stone was careful not to apply this description too generally. Of the banks and ditches which led him to explore Easton Down he wrote:

> The exceedingly narrow base, the shallowness of the ditch itself, and the absence of a hard
> trodden layer at the bottom, together with the absence of post-holes under the banks, all
> indicate that this was of the nature of a boundary ditch and not a cattle or track way.

Additionally, these linear features adjoin with neat connections, not the splayed-out junctions universally observed with trackways of any kind. Notions of a defensive origin can also be dispelled, for one of the features runs down a coomb, the worst position for a defensive barrier.

Other cattle walkways were reported on in 1972 by R.C.C. Clay, at Fifield Bavant and Swallowcliffe Down, where there were Early Iron Age settlements. Clay's evidence came from four trenches placed across linear features there. Their narrow bottoms had been trodden hard, and they cut across the intervening ridge, joining together two coombs. In this instance, Clay's interpretation as cattle walkways also appears the only reasonable one. Linear features are conjecturably categorised now as either boundaries, being usually further differentiated as ranch boundaries or 'spinal linears', as noted, or, though less commonly of late, as cattle lanes. As an example of this restricted classification, C.J. Arnold described his sectioning of a linear feature in 1972 as *The excavation of a prehistoric ranch boundary at Quarley Hill, Hampshire*. Arnold's ditch was clearly associated with the hill-fort, and not with any discernible ranch, and it was definitely not flat-bottomed, instead presenting a difficult and potentially dangerous earthwork to cross (*54*). It displays a carefully crafted profile and is asymmetrical, an unnecessarily sophisticated feature, over-demanding of resources to construct unlike if it were a simple boundary. An example of this type of earthwork runs eastwards from Danebury for 2km and is roughly dug, with no attempt to shape the spoil into recognisable banks, but adequate for boundary marking. Arnold's attempts to date the feature at Quarley were inconclusive.

There have been four major studies on linear features conducted in the area, two on Salisbury Plain, reported on by Professor Richard Bradley and David McOmish

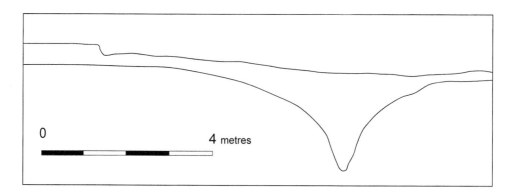

54 Arnold's section of a linear feature at Quarley Hill. *Redrawn after C.J. Arnold*

respectively, in 1994 and 2002, and two on the Danebury environs, the first by R. Palmer published in 1984 and the second by Professor Barry Cunliffe covering research from 1989 to 1996, the conclusions of which were published in a series of reports in 2000 and summarised in Cunliffe's report in the *Oxford Journal of Archaeology* in 2004 entitled 'What cowboys?'. There are differences in interpretation, but all agree on the function of linears as partitioning the land and barriers for stock control. Bradley notes two major phases of construction, from the eighth to the fifth centuries BC, while McOmish favours phases around 1000 BC and 800 BC. Cunliffe considers linears to have appeared much earlier, around 1500 BC, and to have been continually extended until 850 BC; thereafter, up to 600 BC, they often cut across Celtic fields whereas they respected them before this date. He links the latter phase of linear construction to the building of the hill-forts. However, Bradley argues that supposed links between these features and the hypothetical function of the hill-forts are inadequate in explaining the social organisation of the landscape.

Cunliffe observed in his *Iron Age Britain*: 'As with so much of archaeology, interpretation in the end rests with the individual observer and observers are susceptible to fashion.' It is unfashionable at present to consider any linear feature as possessing defensive properties although, as noted above, Hawkes was comfortable with the idea. What has happened since Hawkes wrote is the development of a more sophisticated view of society and its control of the land, one that has no room for the old, simple view of the Iron Age as a time whose main characteristic was seen as inter-tribal warfare. However, by adopting a model without conflict, its proponents have embraced implicitly, perhaps unconsciously, the notion of the noble, docile savage, and that is clearly not a valid or useful description of Iron Age man, or woman – such as Boudica. It is time to heed Cunliffe's general injunction, 'That we should be forced to reverse our perspectives occasionally is a healthy exercise and can sometimes lead to a better understanding.'

There is clear evidence that Danebury and some other hill-forts possessed defensive properties that transcend the prestigious, and have been violently challenged. Danebury's ramparts are described as possessing a glacis slope, steep and slippery, a description accurately applicable to the profiles of some linear features, such as Arnold's, for example. It is not a logical proposition that circular defensive earthworks exist but linear defensive ones do not. Military adventures throughout time have shown the value of defence in depth. Unless defended, a bank and ditch can be crossed, but it is often difficult to do so. Such features make it hard for the enemy to penetrate them, consuming his energies and giving the defenders the advantages of numbers and time. The military express this function as 'a force multiplier', and the factor enters into mathematical equations of conflict. Even small multipliers can be decisive. Ditches, like Arnold's, possess profiles that seem to have evolved as economical of effort in construction while at the same time effective in defence. It is apparent that the design achieved a highly optimal trade-off between the two demands. The glacis slope and ankle-breaking bottom present a formidable barrier: the ditch is too wide to jump successfully. Raiders in a hurry or under attack could lose their footing easily and end up being trapped, injured and vulnerable to annihilation in such an obstacle whose modern counterpart is the barbed wire entanglement. Arguing from a modern perspective that the linear feature was not an effective means of defence is unreasonable. It had to be merely the brainchild of an influential Iron Age commander convinced of its effectiveness to be constructed.

THE QUARLEY HIGH LINEAR

The feature can be observed first on Snoddington Hill, 2.7km north-west of Quarley Hill. It follows the high ground southwards over Thruxton Hill and Cholderton Hill, then it passes Quarley hill-fort 165m to the west, to which it is joined by Hawkes's Ditch 4. The linear feature continues over Boar Knoll and on to Isle of Wight Hill, on its way interfacing with the U-shaped Bronze Age enclosure on Boscombe Down East, thereby forming economically a redoubt on the 'friendly' side. It has been obliterated before entering the woods on Isle of Wight Hill, but was mapped in section there by the author when cut by a cable trench in 1988. Buried remains of the feature were then traced through part of the wood by soil resistivity surveying. The earthwork emerges from the wood extending southwards to Ashley Copse near Lopcombe Corner. Its total length is over 10km. Running roughly at right angles to it, towards the River Bourne, are four linear ditches spaced very roughly at 1km intervals, defining enclaves described without disagreement as 'ranches' of similar areas, each about 3km² in extent. However, on closer inspection, only one of these boundaries actually joins the main earthwork, the others being bounded to the south-east by separate linear features. Hawkes notes, too, that the ranches don't continue up the Bourne Valley to Quarley Hill: there is in his words, 'a marked gap'. It is at this point that the ambiguity of the term 'spinal linear' appears. Some are content to employ it for long features confined to ridges while others require the presence of these 'ribs' of ranch boundaries. It will be argued here that the Quarley High Linear was built with defensive properties, abandoned, and then used – at least in one instance – as a boundary to a ranch occupying land that once lay outside the defended western extent of Danebury's territory. This sequence of events fits with a relaxation of tension or broadening of boundaries in the period from the fourth to first centuries BC, which is suggested by the more widespread distribution of similar pottery styles.

AN EXCAVATION OF THE QUARLEY HIGH LINEAR
AND ITS INTERPRETATION

The excavation of 1984 on the Porton Down Range at Martin's Clump was mentioned in Chapter 4. A 1m-wide section was excavated entirely by hand at right angles to the linear feature. It was emptied of fill and then exposed in profile by a trench cut by hand across it to a depth required by the laid cable, deeper than the bottom of the ditch, thus revealing the ditch's base in profile (55). The preliminary emptying of the ditch suggested it had a flat bottom cut into the chalk but, when the trench was deepened to accommodate the cable, it became clear that the bottom was in fact rounded and had filled with a hard concretion of chalky silt presenting the aspect of a flat bottom (56). This posed the question: how many ditches described as having flat bottoms were inadequately excavated? The published section of Hawkes's excavation of the Quarley High Linear (his Ditch 1) show a flat bottom, a shape that some authors attribute to trampling by cattle, although the narrowness of the ditch makes this unlikely in this instance. Hawkes considered the profile to have been degraded by extensive weathering in the past. Allowing for this loss of definition, and a possible rounded bottom, his profile of Ditch 1 could have reasonably matched that of Arnold's Ditch 3, which resembles the Martin's Clump profile. Differences in construction between the Martin's Clump ditch on the one hand, and the Quarley

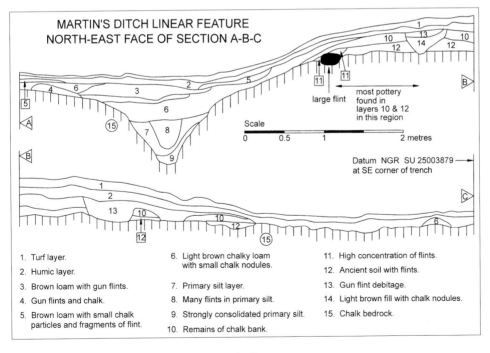

MARTIN'S DITCH LINEAR FEATURE
NORTH-EAST FACE OF SECTION A-B-C

large flint

most pottery found in layers 10 & 12 in this region

Scale
0   0.5   1   2 metres

Datum NGR SU 25003879
at SE corner of trench

1. Turf layer.
2. Humic layer.
3. Brown loam with gun flints.
4. Gun flints and chalk.
5. Brown loam with small chalk particles and fragments of flint.

6. Light brown chalky loam with small chalk nodules.
7. Primary silt layer.
8. Many flints in primary silt.
9. Strongly consolidated primary silt.
10. Remains of chalk bank.

11. High concentration of flints.
12. Ancient soil with flints.
13. Gun flint debitage.
14. Light brown fill with chalk nodules.
15. Chalk bedrock.

55 Profile of the Quarley High Linear at Martin's Clump

56 Photograph of the section of the linear feature at Martin's Clump showing its rounded bottom and the gunflint waste layer

ditches on the other, could be accounted for by the proximity at Martin's Clump of the prehistoric flint mines. There, much of the industrial waste material from the Neolithic flint industry had been incorporated into the bank and used to revet it, producing an inviting accumulation of raw material that had been exploited by modern gunflint knappers, thus lowering the bank, but still leaving a formidable obstacle. From the known profiles, including that fortuitously obtained near Isle of Wight Wood, the Quarley High Linear consists of miles of a consistent and elegantly crafted profile, involving more effort than was needed for a simple boundary feature.

The ditch of this feature, with its narrow bottom, far from being a cattle drove, would have been dangerous to large animals who, if they fell in accidentally, would have been injured – or if placed there to perambulate would have stumbled. The inference is that no cattle were pastured on ground to the north-west of it, where the open ditch was unprotected by a bank. Ground there had been written off. There was no evidence for an ancient hedge on the bank, as is postulated by some authors for other linear earthworks, prompted by their need to account for stock control. The integrity of such a great length of hedge would have been difficult to maintain, and a hedge is only as effective as its weakest point. Bowen reported in 1978 on two sections excavated across a 'spinal linear' at Knoll Down in Hampshire and, on the basis of snail analysis, concluded: 'One can safely say that no hedgerow ever surmounted the boundary at Knoll Down.' Bowen also identified ploughsoil under the bank, with no indication of the abandonment of cultivation before it was constructed. The agricultural pattern had been abruptly violated.

At Martin's Clump the ditch had been allowed to silt up naturally, and there was no evidence of recutting. The primary fill layer had sagged into the ditch, its lip on the bank side being thicker than the opposing one: a natural consequence of there being more material and a longer slope to generate silt on the bank side. The upper curve of the ditch opposite the bank showed marked frost damage, caused by the increased radiative cooling of the exposed, near horizontal surface on clear, calm nights in winter. As silting proceeded, flints fell from the bank, becoming cemented into the ditch by the silt so that, on excavation, a small 'wall' of flints rising for 30cm or so from the bottom of the ditch was found. These features are taken as evidence that silting proceeded undisturbed over a long period. Part of the limb bone of an ox was recovered from the primary silt of the ditch. The initial phase of silting is a fairly rapid process, so the bone found its way into the ditch within a hundred years at most of it being dug. Radiocarbon dating of the bone produced calibrated dates of 245–155 BC (HAR–6801).

The context of the bone and its analysis confirm that the ditch was abandoned, and also approximately when this happened. The conclusions do not accord with those of the major researchers. Cunliffe, for example, would not place the Quarley High Linear later than 750 BC, say, but he writes that it could be shown as having been renewed several times up to the fourth or third centuries BC. Bradley's initial report concluded that linear features are integrated into the landscape of fields and pasture. However, the Quarley High Linear cuts dramatically across the Celtic fields at Porton Down (57), and their violation is noted elsewhere by both McOmish and Cunliffe. This repartitioning of the landscape is now universally accepted as evidence of a major upheaval in society. Bradley sensibly warns against seeking a single reason for the construction of linears, and this conclusion leaves room for the existence of linears that were not originally constructed as *internal* divisions of a unified landscape, but *defined* the boundaries of that landscape, and as such needed to defend its integrity, or proclaim it in an assertive manner, at least. Such liminal features require an understanding separate from mere ranch boundaries, and this does not preclude the 'symbolic' or 'impressive' arguments of those disposed to promote them.

To argue further for the bounding–defending nature of the Quarley High Linear, one needs to relate it to the landscape both tactically and strategically. At the strategic level it can be observed on maps as running from crest to crest along the ridges between them, from Snoddington Hill to Ashley Copse, with Quarley hill-fort as a garrison outpost on the line. Fancifully, one could seek an analogy with the Great Wall of China, but a more apposite parallel might be with a medieval bailey wall with corner towers, with Danebury hill-fort as the castle keep. Military concepts of defence before the modern age remained reasonably constant. Along its length, until it turns across country towards Ashley Copse, it runs parallel to the River Bourne, which raises the question of why an artificial boundary is needed when a natural one exists. At the latitude of Porton Down the drainage basin of the Avon is a wide one, comprising the Avon Valley itself and the Bourne Valley, between which lies a narrow

57 An aerial view of Celtic fields crossed by the later Quarley High Linear feature (top left) in ploughed soil on the Porton Down Range

plateau. Below Salisbury, the Avon receives no more significant tributaries and forms a well-defined barrier. North of Tidworth the valley of the Bourne is topographically insignificant as an obstacle, limiting the boundary width to that of the Avon alone. The bulge in the boundary east of the Avon from Salisbury to Tidworth, consisting of the plateau and its flanking valleys, was probably too small to form a viable, defendable unit, either for the Danebury community or that to the west of the Avon. It was possibly a no-man's-land, ideal bandit territory, a lawless enclave from which raids could be mounted for livestock or slaves. An alternative explanation is that the plateau was indeed occupied by the community to the west of the Avon, who needed to secure the river for commerce by controlling both its banks. The Durotriges, who occupied this territory according to Roman sources, had a port at the mouth of the Avon, at Hengistbury Head, ample reason to control the river well into their hinterland. These two examples do not exhaust the possible speculations, but they demonstrate that sufficiently strong reasons could have existed for the Danebury people to defend along the line of the Bourne over the reach of the bulge.

Tactically, the positioning of the Quarley High Linear, set well back from the scarps of the ridges overlooking the Bourne's valley, militated against a surprise attack. Any raiders would have been denied using the dead ground of the ridge for concealment, needing to make their final challenge across flat, open country in full view of any defenders with time to react to the situation. Perhaps the flat ground in front of the defences was envisaged as suitable for the deployment of chariots stationed at Quarley hill-fort. The positioning of the linear conforms to the account by the historian Tacitus, writing of the German tribes in the first century BC, that they maintained a depopulated zone around their borders. Cunliffe, who has described the Quarley High Linear as marking a distinct cultural boundary in the Middle Iron Age, remarks that if such evidence for depopulation is discovered in the British archaeological record it may be possible to recognise tribal boundaries. The situation at Porton Down offers a case for discussion.

Defence costs resources. The labour of constructing the Quarley High Linear must have been considerable, and by excluding from their territory the slopes reaching down to the Bourne, and many of the old Celtic fields, the community demonstrated that the threat which it was meant to counter was not a trivial one. But the rapid silting up of the ditch, and the abandoning of the construction of Quarley hill-fort, indicate that it disappeared or was dealt with in an alternative way. Unlike the barbed wire of my analogy above, it could not be rolled up and taken away, but with the threat removed, the valuable slopes of the ridge above the Bourne could be utilised as ranches. Within these enclaves may remain the evidence of Iron Age farms and dwellings, and it would be instructive to find them, for few such sites have been discovered in the area.

It is possible that rectangular soil marks near Suddern Warren on the Range may be of Iron Age date, and shards of a magnificent urn, transitional between the Late Bronze Age and Early Iron Age, were found during trenching operations south of the Idmiston Road, at the western end of the Porton Down site. The urn has been restored under the Wiltshire Bronze Age Ceramic Project (*colour plate 10*), but the discovery has yet to be published formally and the urn lacks a proper analysis.

THE END OF THE IRON AGE

The excellent Museum of the Iron Age in Andover displays finds from Danebury and presents realistic reconstructions of features revealed by excavation there. Greeting the visitor is a life-sized model of an Iron Age warrior, armed and moustachioed. But Iron Age spears, slingshots and individual feats of heroism were no match for Roman weapons, discipline and strategy, or irresistible cultural pressures generated by trading in the luxury goods of the Roman Empire. After defeat or capitulation, Mr Moustache and his friends gradually became Romanised – or more so than trade contacts had rendered them already – exercising their authority on behalf of Imperial Rome under the plenipotentiary authority of the Governor of Britain and, like the pigs in *Animal Farm*, became indistinguishable from their masters, even taking regular baths.

The demise of the Iron Age marked a political and cultural watershed, but its economy had inherited sheep farming, which was to persist and develop into a major national feature of agriculture for almost two millennia longer. The next chapter will consider sheep and their effect on Porton Down.

7

Sheep: dung, dew-ponds, drovers and drowners

THE SAXON LEGACY

It must not be presumed that a troop of Romans doggedly clanking their way to Silchester up the Portway, towards the Hampshire Gap, never observed movement on their dextral flank. However, if anything did move on the ground then it seems not to have left an archaeological residue. The Romans came and they went, leaving the country open to colonisation by Angles, Jutes and Saxons. The *Anglo-Saxon Chronicle* tells us that the invaders fought against the indigenous British at *Searoburh*, Old Sarum, in AD 552, and 'put the Britons to flight'. This was 22 years after the Isle of Wight had been colonised and 57 years after the first landings to the south. The campaign had been a long one, and the British had obviously fought hard. Marcus Stone liked to imagine that they buried a roving band of Saxons or Jutes on Roche Court Down on the Porton Down Range.

The new owners of Old Sarum did not incline to the high downland, preferring instead to build their homesteads in the lusher, sheltered valleys, just like the Romans whose settlement is thought to lie nearer the River Avon, but they did exploit the downs for their sheep grazing. This was the time of King Alfred who fought the Danes, and the time of the rise of the great monasteries like Amesbury, founded in AD 973. In lesser places, the Saxons attached their names to their abodes and land charters, and one of them left his spear to be picked up in the area of the Breck in 1991, 100m south of the 'long' barrow. The spear is thought to be a Swanton E3 type, of the sixth or seventh centuries AD, which became the characteristic type of the later Saxon period (*58*).

Settlement in the valley was the rule, but the valley tended to flood, especially with the rise of the seasonal 'winterbournes', which have given their name to a row of Bourne Valley villages lying below the Porton Down Range one of which, Winterbourne Gunner, has parochial lands on the Range. (The name derives not

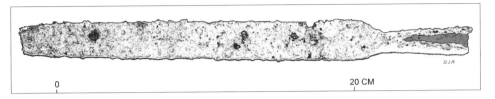

58 Saxon spear head of Swanton E3 type, discovered near the Breck

from artillery but from Gunnora de la Mere, a thirteenth-century lady of the court.) Judicious choice of settlement land was essential. Spurs from the downs run into the chalk stream valleys, and these promontories provided convenient places for farmsteads. One such, in the hamlet of East Gomeldon, part of the parish of Idmiston, its grassy bumps and ruts known locally as 'the humpty field', became a deserted medieval village, referred to fondly by archaeologists as a DMV (*59*). This settlement at East Gomeldon is important to our study because it was from such communities that the downland was exploited and controlled, for the major farming activity was the rearing of sheep, animals that needed the large expanses of the open uplands on which to feed. This particular deserted village is archaeologically important, too, because its excavation revealed the development over the years of the early medieval longhouse, from one where animals lived at one end (in theory) and the farming family occupied the other, into a potentially more hygienic and less odorous arrangement where the animals were banished to separate buildings.

The village was excavated from 1963 to 1968 by the Salisbury Museum Research Committee, and reported on by John Musty and David Algar. It was an agglomerate settlement, as opposed to the later linear villages nearby; that is, its houses did not front on to the village street. Several house-platforms were identified, 'nestling round the hill slopes below the crest on the 225 ft (57.2m) contour'; the plots ranged from 325m² to 555m² in area. Two crofts on the western side of the village, lower down the slope, were associated with buildings. Quite likely, concern for their flooding was not so great as for the houses. Four 'complexes' of buildings were revealed, ranging in date from the twelfth to thirteenth centuries, each holding two or three buildings. Construction was generally of unmortared flint-and-chalk walls resting straight on the chalk bedrock, but the excavators identified one building of cruck construction, where curved, wooden uprights bore the weight of the roof. The settlement lasted for 200 years, with six houses in the thirteenth century contracting to two or three farm units by the fourteenth. It is common but naïve practice to ascribe the abandonment of medieval villages to the Black Death having killed off their populations. However, as Musty and Algar report, the poll-tax returns for Gomeldon, Porton and Idmiston for the year 1377 show approximately the same sums as those recorded 43 years earlier, in 1334. The Black Death did, however, distort the pattern of labour and tenantry across the country, opening up opportunities of economic advantage for

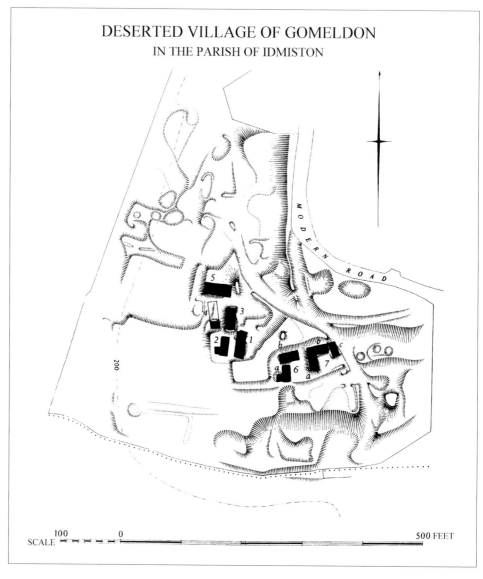

DESERTED VILLAGE OF GOMELDON
IN THE PARISH OF IDMISTON

59 RCHME's plan of the deserted village of Gomeldon showing the buildings excavated. © *English Heritage. NMR. Reproduced with additions courtesy WANHM*

many sections of the poorer classes who survived the epidemic. This pressure and the resulting mobility of the population (if only within the parish), rather than the death by plague of the villagers, may have caused Gomeldon Hill to be abandoned. But the hamlet of Gomeldon still thrived lower down the valley slopes, perhaps around the ancient church of St Mary where house platforms can be seen in the turf.

The general but gradual increase in prosperity and status from villein to yeoman began with processes that can be observed at Gomeldon, for the evolution of the

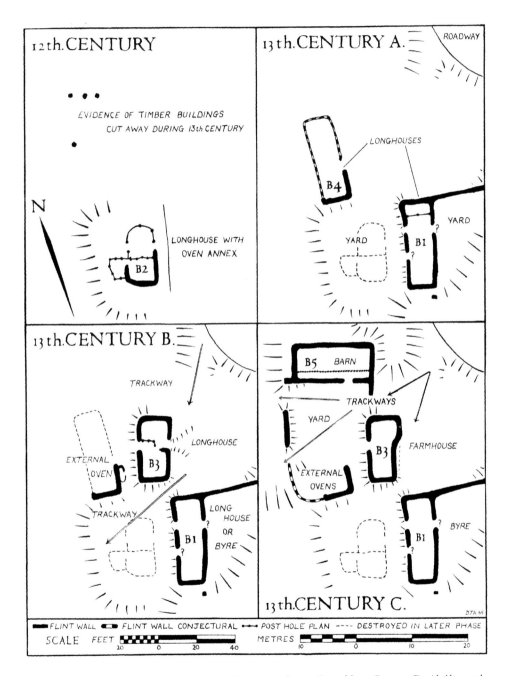

60 The development of the longhouse into a farm complex at Gomeldon. *Courtesy David Algar and WANHM*

longhouse into a separate farmhouse and a barn involved the amalgamation of two holdings (*60*). The economies of scale eventually resulted in the general pattern of a village still evident today, with two or three farms being the norm.

Glastonbury Abbey owned Gomeldon and the manor of Idmiston, an estate of 10 hides. From the Abbey's records we know that in 1518 there were 145 hectares of sheep grazing; an estimate of the number of sheep owned by tenants is about 450. The lord of the manor would also have grazed sheep. Of the animal bones recovered by Musty and Algar from Gomeldon Hill, 70 per cent were of sheep; their analysis suggested that the animals were of the small and slender Soay type, such as those bred in Bronze Age Britain but probably admixed with Roman strains. A pair of iron shears was also recovered from the site although, unlike modern breeds, the Soay sheep sheds its wool in spring.

The early Saxon community buried its dead in a cemetery at Winterbourne Gunner, which was excavated by John Musty and John Stratton in 1960. They found 10 graves, most with grave goods (*colour plates 16-18*), including iron knives and bronze tweezers. There were weapons, too: an iron spearhead, a throwing axe, a shield boss and items of harness. Several Saxons had been buried with jewellery, brooches and beads; two of them had identical pairs of saucer brooches known as Kemble Cross type. Domestic items included a perforated spoon and pottery. The site was excavated again in 1992, for a television programme, when a further 23 graves were uncovered, none so richly endowed as those previously discovered. The second excavation revealed that the cemetery seemed to cluster around a Bronze Age round barrow, another example of the observance of the cemeteries of earlier inhabitants. Radiocarbon analysis of the bones suggests dates between AD 340 and AD 550, a span lying firmly in the pagan Saxon period. This dating, and the dating evidence from the pottery, indicate that the Saxons were firmly settled in the area before the battle of Old Sarum in AD 552, leading to questions about the reliability of the entry in the *Anglo-Saxon Chronicle*. Professor Hawkes speculated that the battle was initiated by the Celts trying to win back Old Sarum.

SHEEP TECHNOLOGY

Before the middle of the fourteenth century most wool was exported, much of it through the port of Southampton, which grew prosperous as a result. But a flourishing indigenous textile trade had developed by 1400, and it was the export of cloth that became important. John Chandler, in *Endless Street*, gives a detailed account of the process of manufacturing cloth, beginning with wool production. One well-documented fifteenth-century Salisbury merchant, John Halle, grew very rich on wool, as evidenced by the magnificent nature of his house, which survives. The splendid medieval churches of the West Country attest to the widespread nature of the wealth created by wool.

However, wool was a by-product, although an important one, of the corn-producing system; the chief source of income for the farmers of the Bourne Valley was their wheat and barley, which they sold at market in Salisbury, Amesbury, Stockbridge and Wilton. The sheep were traded at markets and also at 'fairs', held most notably nearby at Weyhill, although long stretches of sheep droves, such as the Salisbury to Shaftesbury one, now the A30 trunk road, attest to the considerable distances over which sheep were driven for sale. However, even this distance is small compared with the droves reaching into Wales. The wide sheep drove from Porton village to Boscombe Down West is now a minor road, 4.5m in width, but the distance between its hedges is 18m, and the site of a dew-pond on it can still partially flood the road after prolonged downpours.

Numbers of sheep in the country at that time are hard to estimate. The combined manorial flocks may have been between 1-2000 head, perhaps more. Chandler quotes an estimated half a million sheep or more for the whole of Wiltshire in 1794, when they were reared more intensively than before. By 1850 there could have been a million. Sheep farming lasted well into the twentieth century. Before the Second World War, there were some 35 families in the nearby village of Winterslow dependent on hurdle making for a living, a trade necessary for the folding of sheep; after the war the number had dwindled to two, owing to the decline of sheep farming, prompted partly by the increase in arable land necessary to grow food in wartime and post-war imports of wool and lamb. Hurdles consumed considerable quantities of hazel and the remains of hazel coppices are frequently encountered over the downland. On the Porton Down Range, a large area of hazel stools still exists north of Tower Hill, and also a patch on Battery Hill.

The method of agriculture employed in medieval times was termed 'sheep and corn'. The sheep were driven along droves on to the downs in the morning, where they grazed all day. At night they were driven home and folded on an arable field where they released their nutrient-rich dung and urine. The Wiltshire horned sheep (*61*) were said to have been favoured because they held their dung during the day. They were large, heavy animals with a light fleece. They had a rival in the Hampshire Downland sheep, a flock of which was founded in 1890 by Henry 'Inky' Stephens of Cholderton, next to the Porton Down Range, and which is still maintained – the largest in the country – by his great-grandson, Henry Edmunds. The Hampshire Downland sheep originated in the eighteenth century with a cross between the Wiltshire horned sheep and the smaller South Down breed. There were generally two or three fields in a manor, which were folded in rotation, with perhaps one left fallow for a year. The dung-fertilised fields sustained corn crops. By this process, the nutrients in the downland soils were transferred to the valleys. The sheep were left on the downs in summer; this procedure appears to have prevented the downland soils from becoming completely depleted. However effective the method of farming proved, it was highly energy inefficient, for most of the effort of the sheep was devoted to transporting little penny-packets of dung over many miles.

A WILTSHIRE RAM.

Pub.ᵈ 1ˢᵗ Jan.ʸ 1811 by Rich.ᵈ Phillips New Bridge Street.

61 A Wiltshire ram, from Thomas Davis's 'General view of the agriculture in Wiltshire', 1811. *Courtesy Wiltshire County Council Libraries and Heritage*

The sheep performed another agricultural function: flocks were driven over arable land sown with corn broadcast by hand. They trampled the seed into the soil to just the right depth, protecting it from birds and from drying out. The ewes also yielded milk, from which cheese was made.

Every village or manor had its own sheep down on the chalk uplands, marked by boundary stones. That is how the military camp got its name, for the flocks from Porton village had rights to graze on Porton Down. On the Porton Down Range there are downs once grazed by other villages and manors: Idmiston Down, Roche Court Down, Gomeldon Down, Allington Down and Boscombe Down East. Boscombe village had rights to another down, too, Boscombe Down West, lying on the other side of the River Bourne. When the military airfield was built there it was known simply as 'Boscombe Down'. Not all the downs on the Range were named after manorial estates or villages; there are Juniper Down, Thorney Down, Maiden Down and Easton Down.

That irascible and radical journalist, William Cobbett, wrote in his *Rural Rides* of a journey along the Avon Valley from Netheravon to Salisbury in August 1826:

The farms are large, I dare say; because sheep is one of the great things here; and sheep, in a country like this, must be kept in flocks, to be of any profit. The sheep principally manure the land. This is to be done only by folding; and to fold, you must have a flock. Every farm has its own down, arable, and meadow; and, in many places, the latter are watered meadows, which is a great resource where sheep are kept in flocks; because these meadows furnish grass for the suckling ewes early in the spring; and indeed, because they always have food in them for sheep and cattle of all sorts. These meadows have had no part of the suffering from drought this year. They fed the ewes and lambs in the spring, and they are now yielding a heavy crop of hay; for I saw men mowing them, in several places, particularly about Netheravon, though it was raining at the time.

Before looking at Cobbett's 'watered meadows' we shall examine the dew-ponds that watered sheep on the Porton Down Range.

DEW-PONDS: THEIR CONSTRUCTION AND LOCATION

These essential components of the production machine for dung and urine were dug to water sheep, but it has been conjectured that the pond near the Pheasant Hotel at the end of the Range, originally the Winterslow Hut and a coaching inn, was constructed for watering horses travelling the London Road. They are almost universally referred to as dew-ponds, but according to Ralph Whitlock, the late Wiltshire broadcaster and writer, the name was not applied until 1877, the correct term being 'sheep pond'. It is as 'sheep ponds' that they are labelled on the 1773 map of Wiltshire by Andrews and Dury (*62*). Whitlock suggests that 'dew-pond' came from a Mr Dew who made ponds for George III. They are designed for catching and storing rain; dew, deposited from cooled, saturated air, makes an insignificant contribution to filling the pond, some 1-2cm a year at most. Some ponds are over 1,000 years old; one is mentioned in a Saxon charter of AD 825 on Milk Hill, north of Pewsey. But most of those dug in Wiltshire and Hampshire belong to the nineteenth century. Unless refurbished at intervals of between 30 and 40 years, they leak and are useless, and they need completely remaking after 150 years or so. There was a tendency to replace them with wind pumps in the late nineteenth and twentieth centuries. Two such pumps once stood on the Range, one at Old Lodge and another at Boscombe Down Barn. The last pond in Wiltshire was dug by the Smith family of West Lavington in 1938, but the Ministry of Agriculture, Fisheries and Food was still instructing farmers on the best methods of constructing dew-ponds in 1958. By then, of course, corn production relied on artificial fertiliser and not the alimentary products of sheep. The traditional sheep farming method at Porton Down lingered until the early 1950s; Mr Bament of East Farm, Boscombe, had a flock of 800 sheep that was driven out every day; if the Range was in use they were driven back again.

Sheep ponds populate the various downs on the Porton Down Range; each served about 400 sheep, maybe indicating the average size of flocks. The typical diameter is about 20m, and the depth of water some 1.2-2.4m. After a suitable hole was dug in the chalk it was lined with a 15cm layer of clay that was consolidated by trampling and beaten smooth, then covered with lime which was also smoothed after being slaked. This layer was covered with straw and then with 30cm of soil (*63*). Sometimes

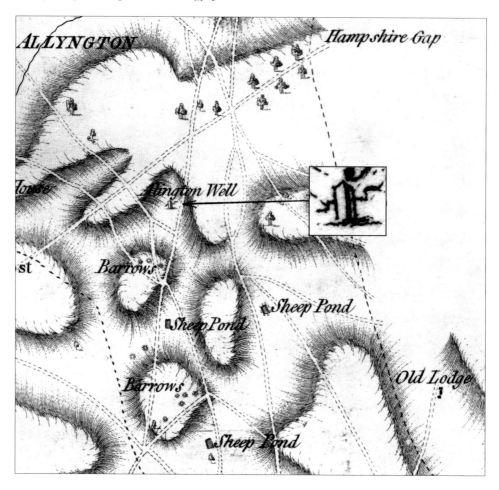

62 Sheep ponds and Allington Well shown on the Andrews and Dury map of 1773 on the Porton Down Range. *Courtesy Bourne Valley Historical Society*

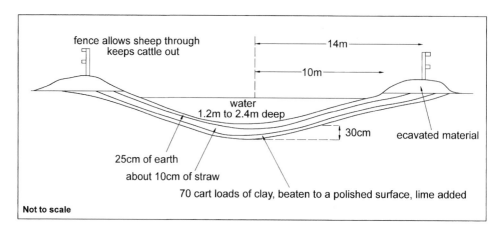

63 Sketch of dew-pond construction. *Redrawn after K.P. Norris*

the clay was mixed with soot or lime to discourage worms from burrowing through it. The pond was enclosed with a fence that allowed sheep through it but excluded the larger cattle and horses whose feet would have destroyed the pond's lining.

The Andrews and Dury map shows three ponds on the Range in 1773, and a two-handled well, but the map does not cover the Hampshire element (*62*). By 1900 there were 21 ponds. Analysis of estate maps and tithe maps by Keith Norris shows that almost every farm in the surrounding parishes had at least one dew-pond on the Porton Down Range (*64*). Some farms had their own 'down barns' located near their dew-ponds. The ponds were constructed mainly in dry gullies, where rain run-off may have been a significant contributor to the fill.

An account of the construction of ponds was given by R.M. Cruse in *Wiltshire Folklife*, 1981-2. The Cruse family was one of two living in the village of Imber on Salisbury Plain who constructed dew-ponds; the Whites were the other. A typical construction charge was £40 each; however, the farmer had to supply the materials and cart away the surplus spoil. The costs had to include wages of 18s (90p) a week for three assistants for four weeks, and lodgings at 2s 6d (12½p) each week if away from home. There was a charge of 6d (2½p) for the removal of every cubic yard of soil (about a tonne) and the same for laying the fill. Joel Cruse was 10 years old when he began to help his father John in the business. They worked at the harvest until the middle of September and then spent six or seven months touring Wiltshire and the surrounding counties building dew-ponds, even venturing into Kent. The

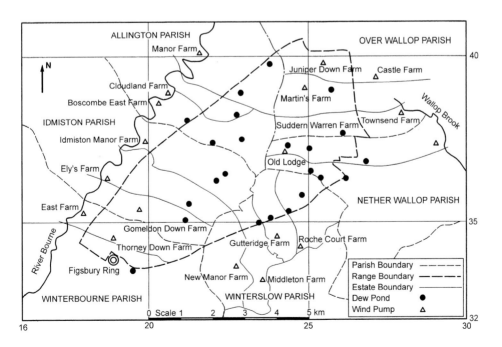

64 A map of the dew-ponds on the Porton Down Range. *Redrawn after K.P. Norris*

labour was too heavy for working during high summer. Unlike his father, Joel did not use a cart: he transported his tools in a wheel barrow.

Cruse makes the point that the bowl-shaped profile of the pond allowed ice that formed on it to crack, and so not fracture the brittle clay lining. The family preferred digging round ponds rather than rectangular ones; they were easier to construct. Myths grew up around dew-ponds, the most obvious being the erroneous one that they were filled by dew. Another claimed that they never ran dry; however, water carts were sent to the River Bourne to top them up when they ran low. Yet another myth asserted that their method of construction remained a closely guarded family secret. In truth, the 'secrets' of construction were well known, one being that the impervious layer extended well beyond the diameter of the pond, under its banks; this procedure enlarged the catchment area for rain while maintaining a smaller area over which evaporation occurred. A 4m 'rim' of impervious extension around the average pond would double its rain-catching capacity.

An old and dry dew-pond on the Porton Down Range was lined with a butyl sheet and filled with water as a conservation project in 1987. It was dubbed Lake Hern, after the then Range Controller, Peter Hern. It has since become a breeding ground for dragonflies.

65 Advertisement of 1892 for Tasker's well machinery. *Courtesy Milestones Museum, Basingstoke*

Several wells were also dug on the Porton Down Range in addition to 'Alington Well'. Charlie and Walter Hobbs, who lived at Gomeldon Down Farm (now Broadfield Farm), are recorded as well-diggers. Some wells at Gomeldon were over 30m deep; the ones on the Range would have been considerably deeper. One of the Range wells was served by a cast-iron hand-operated pump made by Taskers & Sons of Andover. It has been rescued and restored (*colour plate 36*), one of only two known to have survived. The advertisement for it has been traced to a catalogue of 1892; the superior model cost £21 (the chain was extra at 1s 9d a yard, about 9p a metre) and it could raise water from a depth of 360ft (110m) (*65*). Before the well was capped for safety reasons, a colleague of mine lowered a brick down it on a string; the brick stopped at 56.7m (186ft), and this was only the top of the pile of debris that had collected in the well.

THE 'WATERED MEADOWS'

John Aubrey, in his *Natural History of Wiltshire*, written in the second half of the seventeenth century, claims that the Romans instituted water meadows. They were constructed in the valleys of the River Avon and its tributaries in the seventeenth century. Joseph Bettey, in *Wiltshire farming in the seventeenth century*, records an early experiment in water meadow construction on the River Avon at Amesbury in 1624, but the earliest working water meadows in the area seem to have been at Puddletown and Affpuddle in Dorset, and at Wylye, on the tributary of the Avon of that name, in 1632. Bettey provides a detailed description of the construction of a 3-mile stretch of water meadows on the River Avon south of Salisbury, begun in 1665 by John Snow, acting as agent for his master, Sir Joseph Ashe. Bettey's account gives informative transcripts of original documents related to the project and correspondence between landlord and steward. The system rapidly spread up the Avon and along its tributary rivers, including the Bourne up to and including Allington, upstream of Idmiston (*66*). Similar developments occurred in the valley of the Wallop Brook. Water meadows were thus an important factor in sheep farming on the Porton Down Range; without it farming in general in the region would not have been viable against the competition.

The flow of the Bourne was uncertain above Porton, depending on the seasonal contributions from winterbournes, and the complexity of the water meadows decreases as one moves upstream. There are none at Cholderton, where the 'rising of the Bourne' was an annual event, nervously anticipated as much for its potential to flood the village and submerge the roads as for any beneficial effect. (When it does flow, the source of the Bourne is set much further north, at Burbage.) Records kept by the Rector in the nineteenth century show that the Bourne usually rose at Cholderton in December or January and subsided in May or June; differences in

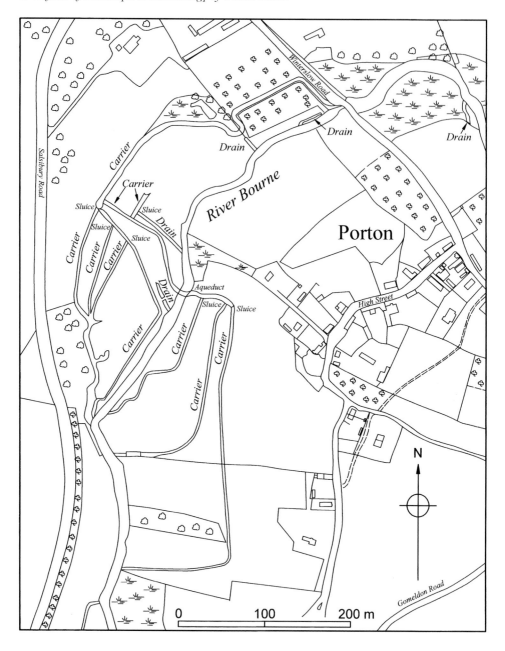

66 The water meadow system on the River Bourne at Porton, based on the Ordnance Survey six-inch map of 1926

these dates are noticeable in his records. Sometimes the flooding was severe, as in 1842 when the Rector wrote:

> For two weeks the road and foot-path were under water from the bridge by the Rectory-gate to the bridge at the corner of the Salisbury-road. So high a flood (with the exception of 'the great flood' caused by melting snow in 1841) cannot be remembered here. The school was closed for one week, and the church could only be reached by the Clump-meadow and Mr. Brown's meadow. The water rose through the floors of two or three cottages. The road was partly flooded up to the end of the first week in March. The coughs and colds which followed have not yet subsided and the attendance at school was much reduced.

Floods returned again in 1904, when the water 'rose to a greater height than could be remembered by the oldest inhabitant', and again in 1915 and 1924. Severe flooding of the Bourne Valley occurred recently, in December 2002, as a result of heavy rain falling on frozen fields. The pressure of water in the higher levels of chalk forced it up through cottage floors in Newton Toney, and the Bourne was contaminated with sewage. Roads became impassable. The River Bourne above Idmiston has often run dry in recent times, even over the winter months, partly owing to the commercial extraction of water having lowered the water table.

Flood control was not the first priority of the water meadow scheme, but it did aim to smooth out variable flows. The system relied on a series of man-made carriers, drains, spillways and leats leading off the main channel and controlled by hatches built of stone. Greensand was the best stone for the purpose, for it could withstand being alternately submerged and dried out without frosting; some of it came from quarries at Fovant. (Greensand underlies the chalk.) For the water meadows to function successfully, the banks of the water channels needed to be kept level to within an accuracy of an inch. Wooden gates in the hatches were raised and lowered to control the flow. The flooding of the water meadows protected the grass from the early frosts and fed it with nutrients. Ample, highly nutritious, early grass was thus provided for the suckling ewes, and several hay crops for winter feed for cattle. Cows were not pastured directly on the water meadows; the heavy beasts would have trampled the carefully levelled banks of the water channels.

Strict rules were needed to govern when the water was let downstream from farm to farm at proscribed periods. Holding on to the water for an extra night when frost was forecast was a grave infringement of the regulations. The maintenance and operation of the system was under the control of skilled 'drowners'. Members of the large, local Hatcher family claim that their name derives from the occupation of their forebears in maintaining the sluices; however, there is no name of Drowner in any local directory. Water meadows were never 'drowned'; the art consisted of keeping the roots of the grass just covered with water, hence the need for the accurate maintenance of the water channels. Constructing and operating water meadows was not cheap, but produced huge benefits to farming. The last working of the water meadows at Porton occurred in about 1937, but the hatches are still operated downstream to control the flow to prevent flooding and regulate the water through a working water mill at Ford. One of the biggest difficulties in creating a water meadow complex was accommodating the needs of other river users. On the Bourne the problems consisted mainly of satisfying mill owners; however, south of Salisbury there were navigational interests to satisfy, too.

It was the integrated management of the land, with the water meadows around the river, the pasture meadows next to them, the arable land farther up the slope, and the downland beyond that, that produced the long, narrow tithings characteristic of the chalk stream settlements. Every farm had a share of these resources, vital for survival and often productive of prosperity.

Changing patterns of agriculture at home, including the use of artificial fertilisers and the increasing competition from New Zealand wool and lamb, saw the decline of the sheep, and hence of the water meadows. Some have achieved new roles as Sites of Special Scientific Interest, as has the sheep's daytime territory, the Porton Down Range.

8

The eighteenth century: the Surveyor General, the surveyors, and gunflint knappers

WILLIAM BENSON

As personalities go, William Benson's was indisputably unattractive. His father was an iron merchant, very rich and indulgent to his son. As a member of the 'new rich', William Benson junior, who was born in 1682, was definitely not an aristocrat: he was, by inclination and social custom, politically a Whig. William was sent on the customary grand tour of Europe, which included Stockholm and Hanover, where he acquired architectural and literary pretensions. Stockholm was perhaps a visit home, for the Benson family originated in Sweden and dealt in Swedish iron. Hanover was a prudent stop for a man who already harboured political aspirations, for in 1701 the Act of Settlement declared that, following the reign of Queen Anne, the succession should pass to Sophia, Electress of Hanover, and grandmother of James I of England. The crown passed to Sophia's son who became George I in 1714, thus founding the House of Hanover. George's succession was only assured, however, when the dying Anne, who had always favoured the Tories, made the Whig Duke of Shrewsbury her chief minister. The way forward for a politically ambitious young man was thus clear: become a prominent Whig and insinuate himself with the Germans who predominated at court. Benson did both.

To ingratiate himself with George I, Benson passed off as his own designs for a splendid and curious waterworks to grace the pleasure gardens of the king at Herrenhausen, the palace of the Electors of Hanover. The fountains and cascades were supposed to surpass in grandeur the best in France; they still exist. However, the design and hydraulic mechanism had almost certainly been conceived by a shy curate from Amesbury, Thomas Holland, who is known to have had an interest in such devices. Hydraulics was an extension of politics for Benson. He owned an estate at Shaftesbury and installed piped water from his land for the residents of that town. This supply he threatened to cut off if they did not elect him their Member of Parliament.

On returning home from Europe, Benson married Eleanor, the daughter of a rich Bristol merchant, Joseph Earle, and took a lease on the Palladian House of Amesbury Abbey, which was built in 1660 for William Seymour, the Duke of Somerset, by William Webb, a nephew and pupil of Inigo Jones. This was to be Benson's temporary abode, for William senior, as part of a £10,000 marriage settlement, had bought for his son, in 1709, an estate with its medieval house at Newton Toney where Celia Fiennes, the tourist and diarist, lived. (It was Nathaniel Fiennes, Viscount Saye and Sele, who conferred a knighthood on Benson's father that year.) William planned to pull down the old house and build his own in the Palladian style. Whigs built Palladian: Tories built Baroque. Palladianism was, like the Baroque, a neo-classical style, but it eschewed the masses of convoluted, exuberant ornamentation that embellished the latter form.

Benson's new estate stretched, just, to Tower Hill on what is now the Porton Down Range. What he did there is the main concern of this story.

Benson served as High Sheriff of Wiltshire for 1710 and became a Member of Parliament for Shaftesbury in 1715. But this was not enough. By spreading scurrilous rumours, Benson succeeded in getting Sir Christopher Wren dismissed from his post of Surveyor General of the King's Works with himself subsequently installed as Wren's successor. Then he obtained, in addition, the posts of Auditor of the Foreign Accounts and Auditor of the Imprest, both were lucrative positions. He was then universally known as Mr Auditor Benson. In all his posts, Benson was overtly corrupt. Eventually, he was dismissed as Surveyor General – but kept the plans of the public buildings he was responsible for, attempting to sell them back to the king, and he was given a large debt from Ireland, due to the Crown, as compensation for his loss of post. He had attempted to pull down the House of Lords, declaring it as unsafe, and refused to remove the scaffolding when he was proved wrong. He and the architect Colin Campbell wanted to replace it, at a profit, with a Palladian structure, another dominant political statement. At the end of his life Benson went mad.

THE FOLLY OF BENSON

In 1710, Benson began building the first Palladian villa of the neo-Palladian revival at Newton Toney, calling it Wilbury, a name that some derive from *Wil*ton and Ames*bury*, but which can also be interpreted as 'Will's Castle' (67). Colin Campbell illustrated the villa in his book *Vitruvius Britannicus*, writing that Benson 'invented and built' it; but it was almost certainly Campbell's invention, although it contained

WILBURY HOUSE
Wiltshire.
The Seat of Sir Th. W. Malet Bart

London Published by John Harris 2 Pauls church Yard May 1 1813

67 The south façade of Wilbury House in 1813 showing the added sub-octagonal flanking pavilions

elements of design from Amesbury Abbey. As was customary for the period, Benson furnished his new estate with subsidiary architectural features: a temple, grottoes and a folly. The dictionary definition of a folly is 'a building in the form of a castle, temple, etc., built to satisfy a fancy or conceit, often of an eccentric kind'. William Benson was certainly eccentric and had many conceits; one of these compelled him to place his folly at the highest point of his estate, now called Tower Hill or Folly Hill, 174m above the present Ordnance Datum. From there, extensive views across Wiltshire and Hampshire were obtained, although tree cover now almost completely obscures the vista. Conversely, people for miles around, including other major landowners, over several generations, would have regarded the monument as a familiar, prominent landmark and been reminded of the self-regard, importance and authority of Mr Auditor Benson.

The folly formed an integral part of the overall design for Wilbury because the long axis of the villa was built exactly at right angles to the line connecting the two buildings. Benson had this flexibility to site and orientate his villa in this way, remote from the original manor house; Lady Sarah FitzHerbert (née Sarah Perrin, whose great-grandfather had once held a copyhold at Newton Toney), writing in her diary of 1792, states that Benson pulled down the old house and built his villa a mile distant from the village. Centrally placed, symmetrical axes, such as were marked by Benson's Folly, as it became known, are common architectural features of grand country houses, with the 'station of view', often an obelisk, visible through the front entrance. This was indeed the configuration until the house was literally turned about, with the rear remodelled in the late eighteenth century to become the front façade. Later still, an avenue was constructed on a reciprocal bearing to that of the folly; finally, an obelisk was erected on this new axis in 1897.

By this time, the folly had been pulled down, or succumbed to gravity, perhaps assisted by the elements. Colt Hoare describes how he saw the folly on his journey along the Portway in 1824; his family connection with Benson (Benson's sister married Henry Hoare the banker and builder of Stourhead House) gave him particular reason for noting it. The map of Wiltshire surveyed by Greenwood in 1819–20 includes the folly, but it is not shown on the Tithe Commutation map for Newton Toney dated 1839. The Ordnance Survey (OS) six-inch map of 1883 records a triangulation point where the folly stood. Particularly strong gales occurred in the years 1822, 1824, 1828 and 1836, and an exposed and badly maintained folly could have been blown down in any one of these incidents. In 1836, heavy snowfalls across southern England produced the first recorded avalanche, in Lewes, Sussex; snowfall is another possible agent of destruction. A letter by a Canadian, Alma Dick Lauder, to her mother, written from Newton Toney Rectory in 1882, contains the passage:

> Yesterday we had a lovely walk to a place called Folly Hill near here, Beautiful beech woods and the fallen ruins of an old temple on top of the hill.

It seems likely from all these accounts that the folly had fallen by 1839.

The site is marked today by a neat, oval mound of soil-covered rubble, of sharp profile, some 21 x 14m and 2m high, the long axis oriented closely east-north-east to west-north-west (*colour plate 19*). The summit of the hill is much as described by John Musty in 1964:

> The site is overgrown with scrub, but a recent examination of the top revealed blocks of stone. These are not of local origin (i.e. Chilmark) but probably came from the Bath area, possibly at the same time as the stone was obtained for Wilbury House.

Contrary to Musty's assertion, Wilbury House contains Chilmark-type stone, from quarries lying about 30km to the west-south-west, but not Bath stone. The stone blocks have since been rolled down the hill; 10 of them lie some 30m to the south-east (*colour plate 20*). They are either too massive to move easily or so specifically shaped that reuse would be difficult. The aspect is of an assemblage that has been robbed of reusable, dressed stone. And so it would appear to have been the case: a resident of Newton Toney, Mrs Joan Hopkins, relates a remarkable piece of oral family history. Her great-grandfather, Richard Zillwood Cooke, born in 1834, remembered going by horse and cart with his father Robert, born in 1800, to Folly Hill to fetch stones for the building of the new church at Newton Toney that opened in 1843–4. In particular the stones of a spiral staircase were recovered. This event occurred when Sir Alexander Malet owned the estate. A check by the author revealed that the staircase in the church has treads with the same dimensions and angles as a tread found on Tower Hill.

A Miss Armstead, a former schoolteacher at Newton Toney who was born around 1900, claimed that her grandfather had seen an illustration of the folly, possibly, she thought, in an old magazine type of publication. However, exhaustive searches for this publication have proved unsuccessful. There is only one indication of what it looked like: a tiny image about 3mm across of a central tower flanked by smaller chambers appears on the Andrews and Dury map of 1773 (*68*). The image is too small to show detail but it is likely to be reliable because Andrews hoped to recoup his costs by selling his map to estate owners whose mansions and gardens he generally depicted with detailed accuracy. Wilbury was engraved accurately. (Many churches are shown on the map in a conventional way, and Andrews mistakenly engraved the tower of Salisbury Cathedral at the west end. Obviously, he was not targeting an ecclesiastical market.) The Wiltshire Building Record describes the folly as 'a circular brick structure', for which no authority can be found, which stands in contradiction to Andrew's pictorial evidence, and which does not accord with the remains on the ground.

Ruined vistas were much in vogue in the eighteenth and nineteenth centuries. Support for the notion that the folly was retained as such comes from the presence of a Turkey oak on the summit. This species was introduced into England in 1735, and the specimen on the summit is most likely to have resulted from a parent being planted there (it, too, has produced a sapling). Turkey oaks were planted around a

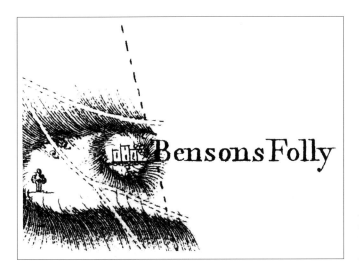

68 Enlarged detail of the Andrews and Dury map of 1773 showing Benson's Folly. *Courtesy Bourne Valley Historical Society*

grotto at Wilbury in the nineteenth century. Isolated Scots pines flank the mound, another indication of a contrived skyline feature. Lilac, a persistent shrub, is still found on the hill, a probable indication that the folly possessed gardens.

Wilbury was built exactly 2 miles from the folly. Such precisely measured lines are of interest to freemasons, as evidenced by the stone they erected in 1967 at Old Sarum to commemorate the measurement of a fundamental base line of the OS from Old Sarum to Beacon Hill near Amesbury, surveyed by Captain Mudge in 1794. Benson was involved in scandalous nocturnal rites on Brownsea Island near Poole, which he had bought, during which screams were heard and a girl disappeared. Ritual was thus a feature of his life. Benson was almost certainly a freemason, and this would account for his unusual preferment and the leniency with which his crimes were dealt. Tower Hill stands athwart the longest east–west line of latitude in England, from St Margaret's at Cliffe in the east to Baggy Point in the west. Mudge's baseline also crosses this segment of latitude. Beacon Hill and Tower Hill are close to the longest line of longitude in England, which is near two degrees west in longitude. The choice of a baseline in this area is sound geodetic practice, for it minimises the total errors inherent in mapping a spherical surface on to a flat map by triangulation. It is more than speculation to suggest that Benson intended to establish his axis as the fundamental baseline for a survey of England. Unfortunately for him, it was too short to be practical, four times its length being needed, at least.

The OS did recognise the value of the folly as a triangulation point, and it is marked as such on old maps. However, the OS maps were surveyed after the folly fell down. An examination of the crest of the mound showed the presence of a square arrangement of bricks (*69*). These were laid on massive stone blocks, presumably originally the foundations of the folly, and had been levelled with slivers of slate. This led to the notion that the bricks marked the triangulation point. Old trig points are recorded in a series of 'guard books' held in the National Archives at Kew. An exhaustive search of the books for Wiltshire proved fruitless, but the entry occurred in one of the Hampshire volumes. The entry is dated 30 December 1865 and reads:

> *Name* Tower Hill, *Parish* Newton toney, *Nearest Town* Newton toney village, *Type* 2.6 stone,
> *Description* A well known hill with a wood on it where a monument once stood – But this
> has fallen down 1 lo. from Old Lodge house.

Here, indeed, was the confirmation that the folly had fallen down. The type, 2.6 stone, refers to the size of the brick platform in feet; Tower Hill does lie one mile from the site of Old Lodge, but the abbreviation 'lo.' is unclear. Some of the triangulation points described in the guard books are ephemeral: one was a bush, another for 'Wilbury Hall' consisted of an arrow cut on a tree trunk. The Tower Hill triangulation point was not used in the Primary Triangulation of the British

69 Brick 'plinth' on the mound on Tower Hill, the triangulation point of 1865

Isles (the establishing of large triangles spanning the country); a separate one was constructed on Thorney Down Hill (now Battery Hill) for this purpose instead. Tower Hill was used for the smaller triangles by which local details were surveyed.

A MODERN SURVEY OF TOWER HILL

As described in Chapter 4, a topographical survey of the crest of Tower Hill was made in 1998 (*31*), together with a resistivity survey by Southampton University of an area 40m square. English Heritage identified a sub-rectangular enclosure some 40 x 35m, which they entered into the National Monuments Record with the name Tower Hill Enclosure. It was to determine the nature of that enclosure that the Porton Down Conservation Group conducted their excavation. Illuminating though the excavation was, it failed to produce a definite answer, and this must be determined at some future date. The survey showed what appeared to be the features of a garden and a pond, overlooking which is an element which may be a promenade area. An area to the south of the mound seems to have been excavated to form a level area, possibly a sheltered lawn. The resisitivity survey produced anomalies that may be footings for walls or steps. The potential exists to determine the setting of Benson's Folly, but the resources are not available at present.

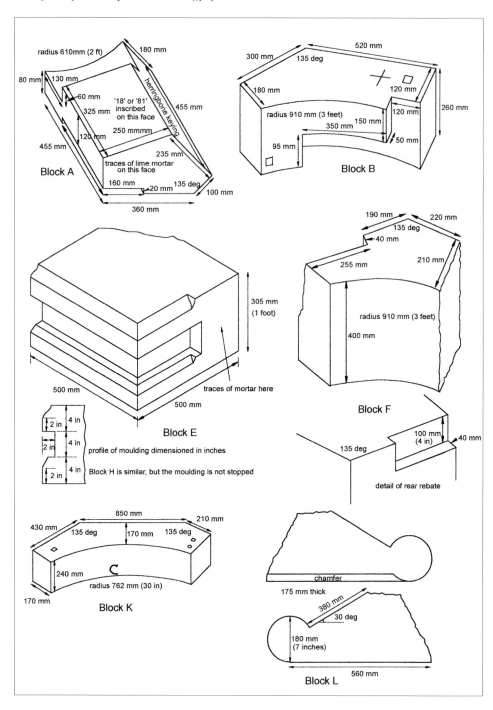

70 Sketches of some of the masonry blocks on Tower Hill

71 Keystone from the doorway of Benson's Folly

THE CONSTRUCTION AND DESIGN OF THE FOLLY

The oval mound of debris was not excavated, but material on the surface consisted of dark red bricks, of an eighteenth-century standard size; fragments of red, unglazed tile; many fragments of limestone; and many flint nodules, none of which were knapped skilfully and none of which bore mortar. Many flakes of flint, knapped with a metal hammer, were found to the south of the mound, suggesting that flint was worked there for building purposes. Knapped flint would have been an attractive salvable building material, for Newton Toney Church is built of such. Debris remaining on the site may thus not be representative of the original structure, and some may have come from ancillary buildings.

All the masonry blocks were measured, drawn and photographed. Sketches of some are shown (*70*). Imperial units had been used in constructing the large blocks. They included the keystone of a large pedimented arch, 8ft (2.43m) in diameter and with an apex angle of 135 degrees (*71*). It has a much weathered boss above the arch that must have formed a decorative, heraldic representation, perhaps of an oak tree. Below the boss, and within the apex of the pediment, is a through hole, slanting back to front. The hole is almost certainly a drainage feature, and asymmetrical fixing holes and recesses on either side of it suggest that it carried a suitably naturalistic or fantastic creature with an appropriate orifice – a cascade or gargoyle intended to drain the central section of the roof. Positioning the cascade over the doorway is consistent with the eccentric features of a folly. Plinth blocks were present, but the most instructive blocks were sub-octagonal in shape (with corner angles of 135 degrees) and circular holes in the centre. The hole in one block was 5ft in diameter (1.52m) and the other two had 6ft holes (1.8m). The two largest had stepped rebates cut in them into which the stone stair tread fitted exactly (*colour plates 21, 22*). The evidence of the blocks is consistent with the illustration by Andrews and Dury: the central tower was pierced by a large archway and it was flanked by two sub-octagonal chambers of unequal size, in the larger of which rose a spiral staircase.

Support for this construction comes from the current aspect of Wilbury. The house passed through a series of owners, one of whom added a pair of sub-octagonal flanking pavilions to the façade facing the folly, most likely around 1790, in what can be interpreted as a deliberate attempt to reflect its elevational aspect (*67*).

The gatehouse design would have appealed to Benson, who was ever anxious to upstage all around him, for it would have presented the illusion of access to yet more of his estate. In fact, it stood close to his boundary and opened on to the Eyre-Matchams' lands. Their ancestor, Giles Eyre, had built a prominent hexagonal brick folly (known now as the Pepperbox) some 13km to the south in 1604, visible from Tower Hill when the tree cover is propitious. Benson's folly was more prominent, grander and dominating. It was not the gentle 'summerhouse' of the Pepperbox, as engraved on the Andrews and Dury map. It was a symbolic instrument of control that sprayed a jet of water on those who passed through its portal in wet weather. Metaphorically, it is what Benson did to everyone!

THE ORIGIN OF THE FABRIC

The design of the folly is definitely not Palladian, a fact that has prompted speculation that it came from elsewhere and was re-erected on Tower Hill. John Bold of RCHME considered the possibility that it stood originally at Amesbury Abbey. He refers to half of a four-centred stone doorhead found at Wilbury (now lost) inscribed '… HIS TOWER 1600'. The resemblance is so similar to the doorhead inscribed 'DIANA HER HOUS 1600' above an extant hexagonal summerhouse named Diana House at Amesbury Abbey that Bold conjectured Benson had bought the building, which had been erected in 1600 for Edward Seymour, the Earl of Hertford, and relocated it on Tower Hill. However, examination of Diana House by the author reveals that its masonry is completely different in style from the blocks on the hill; the latter are far more robust and not at all suggestive of a building the twin of Diana House. However, the occurrence of the doorhead at Wilbury indicates that Benson was prepared to demolish buildings and transport them with the intention of reuse.

Benson's lease of the Abbey survives. Its terms permitted him to demolish two summerhouses, and to replace an old gatehouse that stood next to the George Inn, which is still flourishing, with a 'handsome and convenient gate'. The new gate can be seen opening on to Countess Road. Benson therefore apparently demolished the gatehouse and one summerhouse. Having removed at least part of the summerhouse to Wilbury, it is reasonable to suppose that this grasping man also took the gatehouse. Dressed stone was a valuable commodity, as evidenced by its recovery for use in Newton Toney church.

It was certainly not socially acceptable to approach a Palladian house through a medieval gateway. Henry Flitcroft's survey of Amesbury in 1726 shows the entrance to the old Abbey, through Abbey Lane, as blocked up. The original driveway to Webb's house was flanked by his Palladian gate piers, still standing but relocated near the church where yet another new driveway opens.

The best guess at the origin of Benson's Folly seems to be as the re-erected, possibly modified, medieval gatehouse formerly the entrance to the ancient Abbey of Amesbury.

MAKING THE SPARKS FLY

While William Benson was lavishing his wealth on Wilbury and its folly, and on such worthy literary pursuits as paying a Mr Dobson of New College £1000 to translate Milton's *Paradise Lost* into Latin, poor men tried to earn their bread around him by making gunflints. Workers in the better-known gunflint industry of Brandon in Sussex could ply their trade under cover, having bought their flint at market from the miners who worked in cramped and dangerous conditions, often 10m or more underground. Knapping at Brandon consisted of removing long flakes from the core and breaking them into rectangular sections. This was known as the French method and was efficient of labour and material; one man could produce 3,000 flints in a day with little waste.

Flintlock muskets were introduced into the British army in 1686 (*72*). The percussion cap mechanism was introduced in 1835, but some flintlocks remained in service for a few years after that date. Contracts to supply gunflints were first awarded in the early eighteenth century. Much of what we know about their manufacture was recorded by S.B.J. Skertchley in a memoir to the Geological Survey of England and Wales in 1879. In an experiment, he discharged a flintlock pistol 100 times; it fired on 36 occasions, flashed 25 times and misfired 39 times. These are not encouraging statistics. He noted that a good flint would last a soldier for half a day. British soldiers were issued with six gunflints before going into battle. Gunflints were also used in domestic strike-a-lights, where an action similar to the gun's was employed to ignite a wick.

In the Salisbury area there were no fine slabs of flint from which to make gunflints, only irregular nodules. The technique here consisted of seizing a nodule and either selecting a flat facet for a striking platform or creating one with a single blow. Then a wedge of flint was knapped from this core, rather like the segment of a grapefruit but possessing an angle of about 45 degrees. With a single blow from a pointed hammer about 10mm from the edge, and at an angle of 120 degrees to it, a half-moon shaped

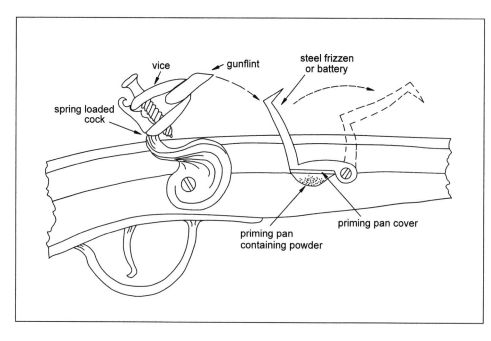

72 A sketch of a flintlock mechanism

flake was detached from one face. There are instances in most assemblages of debris of a different type of core being prepared, which presented two or perhaps three facets from which flakes could be struck. After it was detached, the flake was worked round with iron pliers to make it roughly rectangular, or sometimes chipped into shape. This occurred at home on some occasions, but part-worked discarded flakes have been discovered in the field. The technique of production was termed the Old English method; it resulted in a gunflint with a bulb of percussion that fitted snugly into the vice of the flintlock mechanism, holding it securely (*73*).

Less than 10 per cent of the nodule ended up as a gunflint, so no attempt was made to take nodules to some central workshop; flint was worked where it was discovered, mainly where previous activity had accumulated it. Marcus Stone noted that the gunflint knappers had found the mined stocks of Neolithic flint at Easton Down. Elsewhere on the Porton Down Range they discovered heaps of nodules under a hedge on Roche Court Down, where they had been cleared from an arable field. The knappers' work was visible on Tower Hill, where prehistoric flint quarrying was practised, and in New Plantation and on Isle of Wight Hill. Large quantities of cores, wasters and other fragments appeared in the section of the linear earthwork at Martin's Clump. The amount of waste generated by the knappers was huge: gunflints were produced in their millions. R.C.C. Clay, examining a gunflint industry at Broadchalke in 1925, wrote that 'many cart-loads of these artefacts have been purchased and taken away by the local council to repair the roads.'

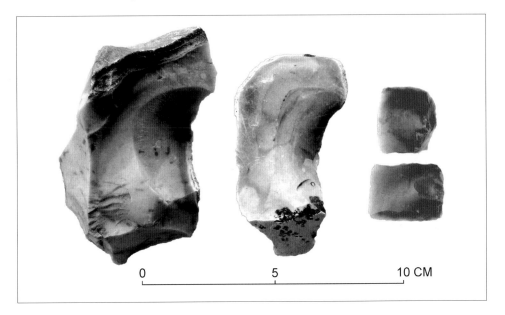

73 Old English pattern gunflints and cores

Some mining for suitable flints did occur in the locality, for John Aubrey, writing his *Natural History of Wiltshire* in the second half of the seventeenth century, comments: 'Excellent fire-flints are digged up at Dun's Pit in Groveley, and fitted for gunnes by Mr. Th. Sadler of Steeple Langford.'

Over 2,000 cores, waste flakes and other fragments of gunflint material were recovered from the sectioning of the Quarley High Linear. The Old English pattern employed there produced characteristic waste cores, generally one large core for every small gunflint, not counting the numerous wasters and other debitage. This waste had been cast to both sides of the bank and left to fall on its crest. It was carried bodily by earthworms into the thick humic layer that had accumulated over the ditch area, and was visible in section as a characteristic bright blue band of patinated cores, indicating the intensity and large scale of the operations there. Some had fallen onto the far lip of the ditch where they could sink no farther. The partial levelling of the bank in this way, and its fortuitous production of a broad, elevated metalled surface, made it attractive as a highway. Two closely-spaced, parallel sets of cart ruts were discovered atop the slumped and depleted bank, each about 1.45m wide, which converts closely to 4ft 8½in, instantly recognisable as the standard gauge of carts and railways. A large horseshoe from the first half of the twentieth century was discovered in the overlying soil, confirming the origin of the tracks.

Martin Fowler, in a *Proceedings of the Hampshire Field Club* report, analysed 40 discarded waste flakes and 70 cores from the assemblage. Some of the cores had more than one flake removed and measurements of the flake scars produced statistics for 83

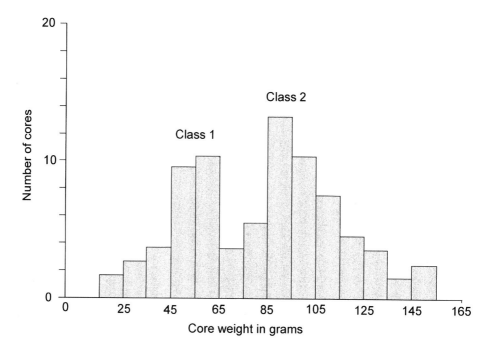

74 Double-peaked histogram of a sample of gunflint cores from Martin's Clump indicating the presence of two knappers. *Redrawn after M.J.F. Fowler*

'deduced flakes'; some of these would have been wasters but the majority produced 'good' flakes. Three linear measures were taken of each flake, also the flake angle and its weight. Similar measurements were made of cores, together with their face angles. The analysis enabled Fowler to demonstrate differences between the industry at Martin's Clump and the one described by Clay at Broadchalke. Two peaks in the histogram of core weights suggested that two knappers had worked at Martin's Clump (*74*). The fingerprinting is quite distinct, even to handedness; in theory it is possible to track an individual knapper across the country as he worked. Such is the forensic nature of statistical archaeology.

9

The nineteenth century
and its legacy

CORN AND CONEYS

The definition of what constitutes marginal land depends on the level of revenue it produces in relation to the resources spent on production. In recent times much marginal land has been brought into productive use by the provision of subsidies, so its revenues do not reflect the land's actual worth within the market. The same distortion of the perceived value of the Porton Down lands was caused by the wildly fluctuating price of corn during the nineteenth century. The Napoleonic wars reduced the supply of corn, as did a succession of bad harvests between 1793 and 1801; in consequence some of the downland was ploughed up for arable farming. Napoleon's defeat in 1815, and some good harvests, removed the pressure on this marginal land and much of it reverted to fallow. But the low price of corn caused an Act of Parliament to be passed permitting the import of corn only when it reached 80sh a quarter (28lbs or 12.7kg in weight). However, it never reached this price, wheat falling to less than half that value in 1822. The call for protectionism from landowners was clamorous but it was matched by demands from manufacturers for free trade. The controversial Corn Laws were finally repealed in 1846, but the price of corn remained high for over 20 years owing to the dictates of international supply and demand.

Three small farms were established on what is now the Porton Down Range in the nineteenth century, on land that had been rated for centuries as only fit for grazing: Martin's Farm (75), Juniper Farm and Suddern Warren Farm. But the raising of corn, on soil that had been consistently robbed of nutrients, in rising, open competition with imported grain, particularly from North America, was a chancy business, and successful farming offered only a precarious and lowly rewarded occupation. Martin's Farm was in a derelict condition when it was taken over by the military in 1941, but the other two were still operating when they, too, were absorbed into the Range.

75 Martin's Farm before it was destroyed by shell fire. *Courtesy DSTL*

Suddern Warren Farm, as its name reveals, was built near the site of a late nineteenth-century rabbit warren. Two other warrens existed on the Range, another example of the use of marginal land. The correct name then for an adult rabbit was 'coney'; 'rabbit' denoted a young animal. Coneys were introduced by the Normans as a table delicacy and have been farmed for their meat and their fur ever since. The rabbit keeps the sward short now that sheep no longer graze the Porton Down Range; only this control of the dominant species produces the rich flora of the chalk grassland, where up to 40 species of vascular plants can be found in a square metre.

PLANTS OF THE DOWNLAND AND WOODLAND

The chief grasses of the downland are sheep's fescue, upright brome, false oat-grass and hairy oat-grass. Plants indicative of old grassland, and which grow in abundance, are rockrose, common milkwort, eyebright and dropwort. The rockrose, together with bird's foot trefoil, horseshoe vetch and kidney vetch, literally turn the Range yellow in July. Other abundant plants are the salad burnet, rough hawkbit, mouse-eared hawkweed, stemless thistle and thyme. Stinking hellebore abounds in the woodlands, sharing habitats with deadly nightshade. Less common plants of the ancient grasslands are bastard toadflax and clustered bell-flower. Wild orchids grow in great profusion on the old grasslands and within the woods, notably the fragrant and common spotted orchids and pyramidal orchid. Particularly interesting or beautiful are the bee orchid, greater butterfly orchid, green-winged orchid and the bird's nest orchid, which is a withered-looking brown plant, a saprophyte living off decayed organic material. Nationally important plant rarities include chalk milkwort, dense-flowered fumitory, candytuft and meadow clary (a Red Data Book plant). Wild flowers abound on the open downland following ground disturbance (*colour plate 23*). Lichen and fungi thrive in the grassland and woodland. Illustrated here is the ecologically important lichen-rich grassland (*colour plate 24*). More than 900 species of fungi have been found at Porton Down, almost half of the known British macro-fungi, uncommon-to-rare species being the earth star, summer truffle and dog stinkhorn.

The Range is home to about 20 per cent of southern England's juniper bushes, 18,000 at the last count. Sheep grazing once kept the grass short enough for juniper seedlings to germinate, but rabbits nibble them. Following the nationwide outbreak of myxomatosis in 1954, which nearly wiped out the rabbit, junipers started to grow again, so that there are two distinct populations of different ages; the old ones are dying now and few new ones manage to survive the rabbits. Large stands of juniper are important because 20 insect species are specific to them, 15 of which live at Porton Down. The juniper also provides a habitat for more than 100 species of insect. The rabbit also wreaks destruction on the ancient monuments and all attempts to control it prove futile.

Scrub forms an important habitat for birds and insects, but it is invasive and needs controlling. In addition to juniper, the main shrub species are hawthorn, blackthorn, dogwood and yew. Woodland, about 10 per cent of the area, is composed mostly of beech, ash, cherry, Scots pine and hazel, with smaller numbers of oak, larch, sycamore, Norway spruce and yew.

In an extensive investigation into grassland types, general flora and the history of land use, including systematic soil analyses, conducted by the Institute of Terrestrial Ecology and published in 1976, T.C.E. Wells and his collaborators identified six types of grassland on the Porton Down Range, five of which occurred on soils with similar characteristics. The differences were attributed to different land use histories, but most grasslands transmute into other types, so there is a time factor involved, too. One agency that assists in this transformation is the yellow meadow ant (*Lasius flavus*), which builds mounds of considerable size, up to 200 litres in volume, and in great numbers (*colour plate 25*). The mounds present micro-habitats with soil characteristics different from their surroundings and so develop a specific flora of their own, including wild thyme and a species of forget-me-not. After a time, perhaps measured in scores of years, the colonies become so large and dense that the ants abandon them; the mounds then acquire a rich flora of lichens, after which the ground cover develops into tussock grassland. One area on Roche Court Down has such a great density of anthills that it is known locally as the 'antscape'. Porton Down Range supports tens of billions of these ants, in addition to a further 19 species, some rare or scarce.

One conclusion of Wells *et al.* was that:

The traditional view that most areas of present-day chalk grassland have been used as sheepwalks for many centuries has not been supported by studies of land-use history, vegetation and soils on the Porton Ranges. Documentary evidence and the plough marks visible on air photographs indicate that over 75% of the Ranges were cultivated. The results of soil studies suggest that some forms of disturbance may have been even more extensive.

However, it was nineteenth-century cultivation, where ploughing on a particular area may have occurred only one or a few times, and farming activities by the military after 1916, that obscured the centuries-old pattern of sheep farming so evident in the division of the Porton Down Range into village and manorial grazing downs, and the construction of dew-ponds. The evidence for extensive sheep farming remains intact.

Wells *et al.* produced composite maps of land use for 1840 and 1856–85 using tithe commutation and OS maps. The former is reproduced here (*76*) and shows the extent to which arable encroached on the former grazing. The later map indicates further encroachment.

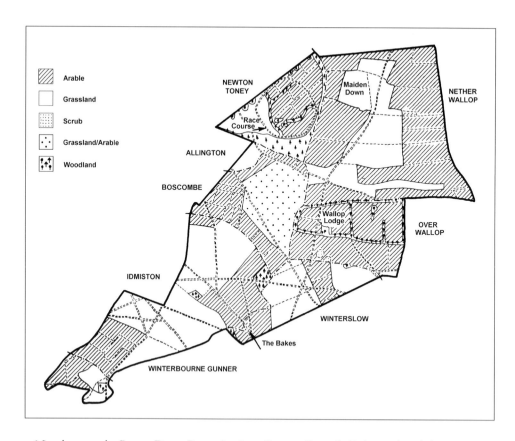

76 Land use on the Porton Down Range in 1840. *Courtesy Centre for Ecology and Hydrology*

PUZZLING FURROWS

Aerial reconnaissance does indeed reveal the pattern of ploughing on parts of the Range, still evident after more than 60 years in some cases. There is one instance of preservation that must surely be unique: from the ridges surrounding the Breck, when the ambient light is just right, long parallel furrows can be observed over an area 300 x 400m. Aerial photographs show them to be far straighter than can be achieved with the normal plough. They must be the result of ploughing using stationary steam engines. These were larger than the usual engine, with horizontal drums mounted underneath them, around which were wound lengthy steel cables, up to 800m, which dragged ploughshares across the fields. Another engine, or an anchored pulley, sat at the far side of the field to handle the return pass of the plough. There is an assertion that steam ploughs were used to detonate unexploded munitions on the Royal Artillery Range at Larkhill, but no documentary evidence has come to light. The Breck lies on the central axis of the Range, and the ridge to the south once bore scars of shelling, but there are no impact craters on the Breck, suggesting that some form of restoration has occurred. Its soils are thin and flinty, unsuited to agriculture. However, in 1918 the Ministry of Supply ordered a large batch of ploughing engines that were allocated to various ploughing contractors to boost the production of home-grown food. Without a ground-penetrating radar survey to search for infilled craters it is doubtful whether we shall ever know if the exciting activity of ploughing up explosives ever occurred on the Breck.

THE ANIMAL LIFE

As one would expect of a large, enclosed area, animal life abounds. There are numerous roe deer, herds of fallow deer, and secretive muntjac deer. Some 16 ancient badger territories have been identified, with a population that fluctuates between about 80 and 140 animals. The large rabbit population supports many foxes, and hares thrive on the downland. Some 100 bird species have been noted at Porton Down, the rarest of which is the stone curlew, there being only 300 breeding pairs in the country. Of these about 6 per cent nest successfully at Porton Down every year, partly owing to rabbit grazing which allows the birds to find the insects on which they feed. So important is the site for stone curlews that about half of it has attracted the European designation of Specially Protected Area, as well as it being a national Site of Special Scientific Interest. Nearly 200 British spider species have been recorded at Porton Down, including the rare *Typhochrestus simoni* found at only two other sites in Britain, making it one of the richest sites for spiders in the country. It is probably the best British butterfly site, too, with 44 species recorded, or 78 per cent of British butterflies. Especially noteworthy are the silver-spotted skipper, marsh fritillary, Duke of Burgundy, small blue and grayling.

Until the early nineteenth century, Salisbury Plain was home to vast flocks of the great bustard. An attempt was made to reintroduce them in the 1970s and '80s at Porton Down but was unsuccessful. Another attempt is currently being made on the Salisbury Plain Training Area.

THE BIG HOUSE

Old Lodge was encountered as a landmark in the OS guard book entry for the Tower Hill triangulation point. In an old estate survey it is recorded that Old Lodge was a new farm of 300 acres (120 hectares) created in 1763 by James Bartlett, who was then the lord of the manor of Fifehead. Until the reformation, Fifehead Manor had been part of the Wallop estate granted to the Priory of Amesbury by Henry II in 1177. The name 'Old Lodge' suggests that some previous building had existed on the site. In 1840 there were two homesteads recorded, Wallop Lodge (Old Lodge) and Old Lodge Farm occupied by the Spyers and Cowdray families, but they are not shown on Greenwood's map of Wiltshire for that date. By 1851 it was farmed by Robert Stacey.

In 1878, the house was in the ownership of Major Robert Poore, who had considerably enlarged it, in the process pulling down an old chapel that may have been erected by a previous owner, the Rev Thomas Spyers. It became a grand country house, with a gymnasium and a Turkish bathroom (*77*). The Poores claimed descent from Bishop Poore, who built Salisbury Cathedral, and they were well connected with the aristocracy. House parties and shooting parties were common, and an ice house was used to store the mountains of game thus shot and recorded meticulously in Robert Poore's diaries in a tiny but legible hand. But the Poore family were philanthropic, too.

77 Old Lodge House. *Courtesy DSTL*

Mrs Nina Poore started the Winterslow Weaving Industry in 1884 to help supplement the incomes of the poorer residents. Winterslow cloth was exhibited in the Albert Hall, and Queen Alexander bought lengths of it. Major Poore started the Winterslow Land Court, a forerunner of local government, in 1892. They bought up land and leased it for 999 years to villagers, who could then build their own houses. In the 1930s Richard Poore, Major Poore's son, arranged for a piped water supply to Winterslow, which was opened in 1935 by his sister, the Duchess of Hamilton. Nina Poore had married the Duke of Hamilton in the church at Newton Toney in 1901. In a nicely symmetrical arrangement, her brother Richard married the Duke's sister.

Nina was regarded as being eccentric. She was devoted to her dogs, of which she owned about 40. Some of these are buried in a pets' cemetery at Old Lodge, with appropriate headstones, one of which is inscribed 'Dear beautiful Pello, taken at Pretoria June 1900, died 29th October 1904'. This dog must have been acquired by Nina's other brother, Robert, when he was Provost Marshal in South Africa during the Boer War. Another South African reference is found on the headstone to 'Matabelle & Peggy'; Robert went with his regiment to Matebeleland in 1896 to put down a rebellion of the Ndebele tribes. Nellie, Stumps, Wee-wee, Totoo, Chick, Zeta and Silver are also commemorated by headstones (*colour plates 26-32*). A favourite race horse, Wilbury, who died in 1907, is buried in Isle of Wight Wood with a fenced grave and a headstone, too (*colour plate 33*).

Richard's brother Robert (1866–1938) was a great sporting personality, as well as a successful soldier who rose to the rank of Brigadier General and commanded the 7th Hussars; his father had commanded the 8th. He served with Kitchener, Roberts, Haig and Baden-Powell. He played test match cricket; his prowess at the game and his tall stature earned him the name of 'the Army's Grace'. His sixth-wicket partnership with E.G. Wynyard of 411 runs, in a match lasting just over four hours between Hampshire and Somerset at Taunton in 1899, still stands in first-class cricket. That year, his batting average was 91.23 runs, a figure only surpassed by Don Bradman in 1930. He excelled at riding, swordsmanship, polo, tennis, squash and shooting.

The wooded rides on Isle of Wight Hill were well suited to horse riding, but a racecourse existed on the Range, on the Wilbury Estate but lying south of the railway line (*78*). Part of it is now referred to as Happy Valley; this is the name of the racecourse in Hong Kong, and was probably applied to the Porton Down course by a military man who had served in the former colony.

Old Lodge was pulled down in 1924 after being bought by the War Office during the First World War. Gypsies had begun to squat there and it had become unsafe. Its materials were used in the construction of houses elsewhere: White Lodge in Church Road, Idmiston, is said to have incorporated its remains. Today, all that can be seen of Old Lodge are the foundations of the house and farm buildings. The once smartly clipped yew hedge that surrounded it is now a large black tunnel, although having been cut back severely at least twice. Some members of the Conservation

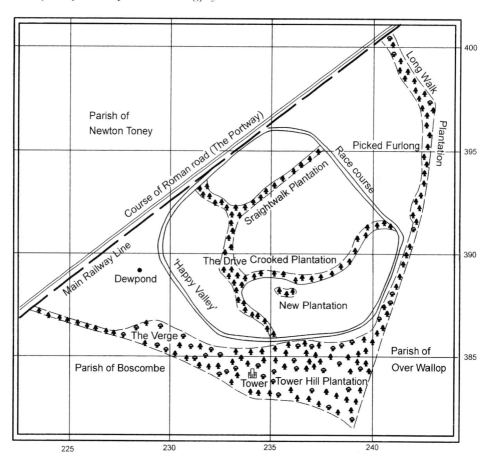

78 The Racecourse. *Redrawn from K.P. Norris*

Group excavated the old rubbish tip, and with great patience assembled interesting items of porcelain that once graced the tables of Old Lodge (*colour plate 34*).

After a gale blew down trees in 1990, a strange little iron cart 45cm in length was discovered under the roots of one of them, which was about 90 years old. It must be one of the few archaeological artefacts excavated with a chain saw. Following much research, it was identified as a night-soil bucket, probably pushed in and out of a hatch in the outside wall of a privy by some lowly servant (*colour plate 35*). Presumably, a more convenient method of disposal was installed at the turn of the century and the wheelie bucket buried. The Prince of Wales invited Thomas Crapper to furnish the royal homes with his stylish porcelain sanitary ware in 1880, and the gentry rapidly followed suit, in what might justly be termed a chain reaction.

10

Latter days

THE BUILDING OF THE CAMP AND ITS LIGHT RAILWAY

The initial assessment of the requirements of the War Department Experimental Ground called for two wooden huts. However, the Camp grew rapidly to employ over 1000 people. In time, it possessed all the facilities of a village: houses, a shop, a post office, a school, a church, a cinema and its own railway. Then, over a period of a score of years or so, the village disappeared: it became a DMV, a deserted *modern* village. No Oliver Goldsmith catalogued its demise in verse, and the historians hardly noticed. The reason for this unnoticed decline is that the rationale for Porton Down's existence remained intact; the fabric of the village was dispersed among the laboratories, administration blocks, workshops and barracks of a military camp and government scientific establishment, all of which proclaimed their permanency. To the outside world the Camp still existed, but the societal apparatus of a domestic community dissolved, and recrystalised where many of the Camp's workers had always lived, in Salisbury city, where a new Ministry of Defence housing estate was built, and in the surrounding villages. Houses and community buildings were demolished or reused for work-related purposes. The decline happened slowly, like growing old, so that it seemed natural and inevitable. It was, however, the result of a planned transition from military to civilian management, with the gradual elimination of what had effectively been a garrison township.

The major instrument of growth of the Camp had been the light railway. The entrance by road lay through the Idmiston railway arch, low and restrictive. All the approach roads into Porton Down were badly surfaced and narrow. Supporting their old ally, units of the Portuguese army were employed to construct abutments and revetments to what were essentially trackways to Idmiston, to stop vehicles rolling into a chalk quarry and the River Bourne. But most traffic came by rail. The Porton Down light railway was a 24in gauge line running between North Camp Headquarters and the main line station of Porton, on the London and South

79 Four locomotives of the Porton Light Railway. *Courtesy DSTL*

80 The Porton Light Railway where it met the main line station of Porton. *Courtesy DSTL*

Western Railway, where a 3-ton crane transferred loads to the narrow gauge wagons. Chief among the first consignment of supplies were 100 chlorine gas cylinders. The line was extended into the Headquarters area, serving every major facility there, and to the magazine. It carried workers, mostly Salisbury dwellers, from Porton Station into the Camp. It was extended from North Camp to South Camp at Winterbourne Gunner, and there were plans to lay lines to the major firing points at Figsbury Ring and Battery Hill, but the Armistice intervened in 1918 and the project was not completed. At the peak of its operation the railway employed five steam locomotives and one petrol-driven locomotive, and 150 wagons of varying designs for different functions, including six open-sided passenger carriages (*79*). The total length of the line was 13km.

The building of the railway saw, after a gap of 2,500 years, moustachioed warriors digging linear features into the chalk in the name of defence. But the cuttings were shallow, the line following the natural contours of the ground and taking the gentlest gradients for the most part. Instead of embankments, trestle viaducts of timber were constructed at Porton Station (*80*) and at Winterbourne Gunner, the latter stretching for 600m and reaching 5m in height. As a consequence of the ephemeral nature of the wooden trestles, and the shallowness of the cuttings, little of the railway can be traced in the archaeological record. During the First World War, the railway transported some 39,000 shells and 6,000 bombs, all for experimental purposes. It ceased operations in the 1950s. The railway was fully documented and illustrated by K.P. Norris in 'Porton Military Railway' in *Industrial Rail Record 48* (1997).

One very durable monument from the early days is the Headquarters Building, begun in 1918. It was erected by Royal Engineers, who did not see themselves as bricklayers. They used a method of construction employed for centuries by the cob wall builders of the locality: wooden shuttering was put in place and concrete, instead of puddled chalk, poured into it. The 'Admin Block' is now a Grade II listed building described as 'of colonial design' (*colour plate 37*); it is elegant in proportions and is graced by a clock tower. Interior alterations are difficult to make: the concrete used in the construction was of a high quality.

THE CIRCULAR GAS TRENCHES

The one concept uppermost in military minds in 1916 was trench warfare, where lengthy lines of dug-in defences faced each other in awful stalemate. The problems for both sides were how to repulse the enemy and how to penetrate his entrenchments. Porton Down was conceived with these aims in mind. The big idea was to dig circular trenches there so that chlorine and other gases could be released at the centre, and gas concentrations measured at some point within them regardless of the wind direction at the time of the experiment, thereby determining the levels

81 The circular gas trenches. *Courtesy DSTL*

of defence necessary, and the weight of chemicals needed for effective offensive attacks. Two concentric rings of trenches were dug in 1916 in an area known as the Bowl of the Range, on Idmiston Down, one of diameter 200 yards (183m) and the other twice this measurement, 3m deep (*81*). Contractors well known to the War Department were employed initially: Messrs Chivers of Devizes. The winter of 1916 was severe; when it was over, the unsupported sides of the trenches had collapsed. Undeterred, the Commandant ordered that they be revetted in timber, which was done in a most workmanlike manner, not at all like the trenches on the Western Front that feature in old films of the war. Adjacent to the circular trenches stood Gas Wood, used for storing the chlorine cylinders. It was later utilised as a target area; it had disappeared by 1938 but continued to be shown on maps for another 10 years (*82*).

When all was ready, it dawned on the military and scientific staff that the effective ranges of the chemicals employed could be measured in miles, not in hundreds of yards, and the facility was abandoned after only a little use. It could yield data of only limited value. Perhaps this limitation could have been foreseen, but the military mind had been conditioned by two years of trench warfare, and once a committee decision had been made it was difficult to modify, especially when the trenches provided much of the case for establishing Porton Down, to which resources had already been committed. (Another such huge, circular, white elephant that lumbered inexorably with unstoppable momentum along the corporate road to completion

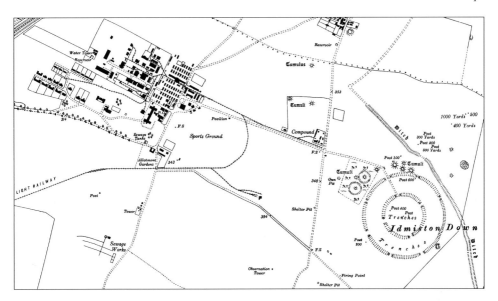

82 The Ordnance Survey six-inch map of 1926 (sheets 30 SE and 61 SE) showing the light railway at North Camp, the circular gas trenches and nearby archaeological features. *Courtesy Wiltshire County Council Libraries and Heritage*

83 The artillery trenches. *Courtesy DSTL*

was the Millennium Dome.) Reason suggests that, instead of constructing a static source position and nearly 2km of trenches, most stretches of which would not be used, it would be more economical and flexible to build a small trench and position the source according to the wind direction and distance being investigated. Contemporary thinking, however, was focused on the large-scale use of commercial gas cylinders, which are difficult to move and position in great numbers. This was in spite of the fact that it was clear by then that the industrial capacity of the country could not sustain repeated chlorine attacks and the effort involved in mounting such attacks against protected troops, who expected them and monitored their adversary's movements, was not justified. Reason did prevail, and the small Artillery Trenches were constructed 500m to the west of the circular ones (*83*), and lying on the axis of the Figsbury range, which is described below. More trenches, known as the Gas Trenches and containing dug-outs, were constructed 700m south of the present Headquarters building to investigate the clearance of gasses from them. Other trenches, the Shell and the Tractor Trenches, were constructed in the Bowl of the Range.

For many years, the Ordnance Survey marked on their one-inch to the mile maps the site of the circular trenches with a symbol almost identical to that used for bivallate hill-forts. Several old Portonians remember being asked by friends where this hill-fort stood, and why was it not on a hill. Mistaken identity this may have been, but the trenches are now, like many hill-forts, a Scheduled Monument, although they present but faint traces in the ground.

THE ARTILLERY RANGES

An experimental artillery range consists of a Firing Point (FP), a surveyed bearing along which the gun is sighted, an impact area or target, and often a fixed Observation Post (OP) from which to observe the impact. The FPs at Porton Down are ideally placed, being elevated and at the edges of the site. This suggests that the need for flat terrain on which to construct the gas trenches was not the sole criterion for the choice of location. The 1929 map of the experimental ground (*84*) shows three ranges. The FP of the first established range, with hard standing and sheds for the guns, stood on Battery Hill, from whence derives the present name. Its axis passed over the Artillery Trenches, on which the guns delivered fire from 60-pounder shells and 4.5in and 5in howitzers. The range from Battery Hill proved to be too short for some purposes, so another FP was established adjacent to and east of Figsbury Ring. The concrete hard standings for the guns may be seen still, and are visible in *colour plate 1*. Here, too, stood gun sheds, and a raised and roofed observation platform. Each gun had its own shed and was moved to its position on rails; there were at least nine such gun positions. The axis of fire ran straight down

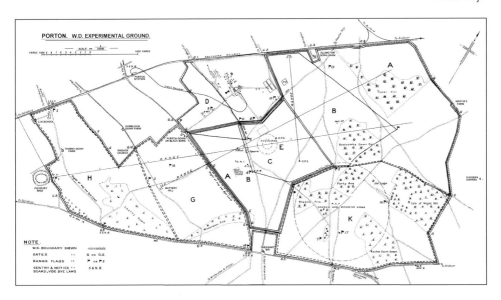

84 The 1929 military map of the Porton Down Range

the middle of the Range, in the direction of Martin's Farm, which is probably why it was destroyed by shelling when the Range boundary was extended. The axis, which was originally marked with range boards at 100-yard intervals, passes over the centre of the circular gas trenches, indicating that not just cylinders were to be discharged at the centre but that gas shells were to be directed there, too. The Figsbury FP was used for 18- and 60-pounder shells, and with 6, 8 and 9.2in howitzers, mostly charged with chemicals and smoke. Sometimes, when greater range was needed, the guns were fired from outside the Range, from land at Malthouse, along the Figsbury axis towards Laverstock, at St Thomas's Bridge.

A further range is shown on the 1929 map, from Gate 2 to OP 6, but there were many temporary ranges used for specific purposes. An important feature was the substantial Trench Mortar Range with its FP at South Camp, Winterbourne Gunner, firing towards Thorney Down Wood. Trench mortars were examples of 'area effect weapons': they could deliver large quantities of chemical agents or smoke over short distances with an accuracy that was low but sufficient for effect (*85*). After the First World War, the Royal Artillery Detachment which had been located at North Camp moved to South Camp, which then became known informally as the Artillery Camp, but they moved back again in 1925 when the Army Chemical Warfare School opened at Winterbourne Gunner. A circular bombing range known as K Range, for use by the Royal Air Force, was constructed towards Roche Court Down.

Travellers could take their bearings from the prominent Benson's Folly on Tower Hill before 1839. Then, after a gap of 99 years, two huge concrete blocks, known as the Hard Targets, were built on the ridge and used as bombing targets by the RAF.

COMPLETE LIVENS EQUIPMENT 1918

85 The trench mortar designed by Captain Livens. *Courtesy DSTL*

One of these was taken down some time after 1949, but the effort and expense was so great that the other was left standing. This is now the landmark for the Porton Down Range, visible from many miles around and likely to remain so for years to come.

11

Final impressions

I first arrived at Porton Down in 1962 as a meteorologist. The Meteorological Division there was internationally renowned for its research into the dispersion of pollutants in the atmosphere. One of its researchers in the 1950s, Frank Pasquill, produced a simple mathematical formula for estimating concentrations of air pollutants that is still in global use amongst environmental organisations and air quality monitoring agencies. It seemed that no weatherman (yes, all men) could become Director of the Meteorological Office without having served a term as Superintendent of the Meteorological Division at Porton Down. My tasks were much humbler. I would forecast the weather for the day and brief interested parties, learning to enjoy the good natured but critical humour well known to weather forecasters, then I would climb into an old, environmentally green van and drive off to the Range with instruments to measure wind speeds and air temperatures. Over the course of three years I got to know and love the Range. Then, I was posted to other regions needing meteorological attention. Ten years later, in 1975, I returned. Lots had changed in the scientific world, but the Range was much the same. Stone curlews still returned in the spring when the green and purple flowers of the stinking hellebore had faded. Maverick primroses still persisted in blooming in January in sheltered spots. The orchids outdid the Chelsea Flower Show. The rabbit population had exploded.

Conservation at Porton Down received a great boost with the arrival of a new Head of Range Section in 1982: David James was particularly interested in archaeology and I got my first chance to excavate there, indulging in the practicalities of a long-standing hobby. Enlightened management encouraged the public to visit in groups guided by experts. Many hundreds have been conducted round the Range on natural history tours by specialist guides. I have guided some 100 parties associated with archaeology and history, over 1,500 people; almost without exception they were entranced by the place, displaying awe and confessing wonder at the richness of the landscape and its timeless aura. Some would pick up a worked flint, knowing that they were the first human to handle it for over 3–4000 years. Others had to be dragged away from the splendid vistas that stretch over great swaths of Hampshire and Wiltshire. Some would linger to breathe in the evening perfume of trampled wild herbs as they strained to hear the long departed dogs barking on the once immaculate lawns of Old Lodge, now thick with the leaves of primroses and cowslips. 'It's Shangri-la,' was a familiar comment. One wrote of his pleasure: 'I wish you could have experienced the warmth of appreciation that welled up after this visit. I, for one, shall never forget it.'

Psychologists tell us that everyone has their personal magic mountain: mine is Tower Hill. There, stood a lost castle, spirited away by the winds, built by the mad and wicked Benson. On its slopes one can scrabble in the dirt of Stone Age folk, who fashioned the means of existence from the gnarled and raw flints beneath their feet, their big secrets – maybe they, too – still lying within the hill. Roe deer peek shyly at intruders. Nightingales sing on its slopes in May, in concert with the haunting cries of distant stone curlews, while mewing buzzards soar overhead in lazy, deadly circles. As I climbed Tower Hill one day in winter, precipitation commenced – in meteorological parlance. Rain fell behind me, snow ahead. I had discovered the magic isotherm. For a meteorologist, that represents true liminality.

Selected Bibliography and References

Abbreviations

PHFC = Proceedings of the Hampshire Field Club Archaeological Society
PPS = Proceedings of the Prehistoric Society
RCHME = Royal Commission on Historical Monuments, England
WANHM = Wiltshire Archaeological and Natural History Magazine
BVHS = Bourne Valley Historical Society

Barber, M., Field, D. and Topping, P., *The Neolithic flint mines of England*, RCHME, English Heritage, 1999
Bold, J. (with John Reeves), *Wilton House and English Palladianism*, HMSO, 1988
Bowen, H.C., *Ancient Fields: a tentative analysis of vanishing earthworks and landscapes*, British Association for the Advancement of Science, 1978
Bristow, C.R., Mortimore, R.N. and Wood, C.J., 'Lithostratigraphy for mapping the chalk of Southern England', *Proceedings of the Geological Association 109*: 293-315, 1997
Butler, C., *Prehistoric Flintwork*, Tempus, 2005

Carter, G.B., *Chemical and biological defence at Porton Down 1916-2000*, The Stationery Office, 2000
Chandler, J.H., *Endless Street*, Hobnob Press, Salisbury, 1983
Cunliffe, B., *Danebury Hillfort*, Tempus, 2003

Ellison, A., 'The Bronze Age Settlement at Thorny Down: pots, post-holes and patterning', *PPS 53*: 385-92, 1987

Fowler, M.J.F., 'A gun-flint industry at Martin's Clump, over Wallop, Hants', *PHFC 48*: 135-42, 1992

Green, M., *A Landscape Revealed: 10,000 years on a chalkland farm*, Tempus, 2000

Hawkes, C.F.C., 'The excavations at Quarley Hill 1938', *PHFC 14*: 136-94, 1939

Norris, K.P., *The life and works of Dr J.F.S. Stone*, MS in the archives of the BVHS, 1994

Palmer, R., *Danebury: an Iron Age hillfort in Hampshire*, RCHME, 1984

Ride, D.J. and James, D.J., 'An account of an excavation of a prehistoric flint mine at Martin's Clump, Over Wallop, Hampshire, 1954-5', *PHFC 45*: 213-19, 1989

Ride, D.J., 'Excavation of a linear earthwork and flint mines at Martin's Clump, Over Wallop, Hampshire, 1984', *PHFC 53*: 1-23, 1998

Ride, D.J. and Hopson, P.M., 'The distribution of flint mines on Porton Down', *PHFC 56*: 266-68, 2001

Ride, D.J., 'The excavation of a cremation cemetery of the Bronze Age and a flint cairn at Easton Down, Allington, Wiltshire, 1983-1995', *WANHM 94*: 161-76, 2001

Ride, D.J., 'Tower Hill, Newton Toney, Wiltshire: prehistoric flints, an early eighteenth-century folly, and the Ordnance Survey', *WANHM 98*: 128-42, 2005

Stevens, F. and Stone, J.F.S., 'The barrows of Winterslow', *WANHM 48*: 174-82, 1938

Stone, J.F.S., 'Easton Down, Winterslow, S. Wilts, flint mine excavation 1930', *WANHM 45*: 350-65, 1931

Stone, J.F.S., 'A settlement site of the Beaker period on Easton Down, Winterslow', *WANHM 45*: 366-72, 1931

Stone, J.F.S., 'Saxon interments on Roche Court Down, Winterslow', *WANHM 45*: 568-99, 1932

Stone, J.F.S., 'Excavations at Easton Down, Winterslow, 1931-1932', *WANHM 46*: 225-42, 1933

Stone, J.F.S., 'A Middle Bronze Age urnfield on Easton Down, Winterslow', *WANHM 46*: 218-24, 1933

Stone, J.F.S., 'Skeleton found in a barrow', *WANHM 46*: 387-88, 1934

Stone, J.F.S., 'A flint mine at Martin's Clump, Over Wallop', *PHFC 12*: 177-80, 1934

Stone, J.F.S., 'A case of Bronze Age cephalotaphy on Easton Down, Winterslow', *WANHM 46*: 563-67, 1934

Stone, J.F.S., 'Three Peterborough dwelling pits and a doubly-stockaded Early Iron Age ditch at Winterbourne Dauntsey', *WANHM 45*: 55-67, 1934

Stone, J.F.S., 'Excavations at Easton Down, Winterslow, 1933-4', *WANHM 47*: 68-80, 1935

Stone, J.F.S., *Notes on excavations, vol 2*, MS in library of Salisbury and S. Wilts Museum, 1935

Stone, J.F.S., 'A Late Bronze Age habitation site on Thorny Down', *WANHM 47*: 466-89, 1937

Stone, J.F.S., 'An enclosure on Boscombe Down East', *WANHM 47*: 466-89, 1937

Stone, J.F.S., 'An Early Bronze Age grave in Fargo Plantation near Stonehenge', *WANHM 48*: 357-70, 1938

Stone, J.F.S., 'The Deverill-Rimbury settlement on Thorny Down, Winterbourne Gunner, S Wilts', *PPS 7*: 114-33, 1941

Stone, J.F.S., 'A Beaker interment on Stockbridge Down, Hampshire, and its cultural connexions', *The Antiquaries Journal 28*: 149-56, 1948

Stone, J.F.S., A decorated axe from Stonehenge Down', *WANHM 55*: 30-33, 1953

Stone, J.F.S., *Wessex before the Celts*, Thames and Hudson, 1958

Stone, J.F.S., The use and distribution of faience in the Ancient East and Prehistoric Europe', *PPS 22*: 37-84, 1956

Stone, J.F.S. and Hill, N.G., 'A Middle Bronze Age site at Stockbridge, Hampshire', *PPS 4*: 249-57, 1940

Stone, J.F.S. and Hill, N.G., 'A round barrow on Stockbridge Down', *Antiquaries Journal 20*: 39-51, 1940

Wells, T.C.E., Sheail, J., Ball, D.F. and Ward, L.K., 'Ecological studies on the Porton Ranges: relationships between vegetation, soils and land-use history', *Journal of Ecology 64*: 589-626, 1976

Woodward, A.B. and Woodward P.J., 'Topography of barrow cemeteries in Bronze Age Wessex', *PPS 62*: 275-91, 1996

Index

Numbers in bold refer to colour plates.

If you are interested in purchasing other books published by Tempus,
or in case you have difficulty finding any Tempus books in your local bookshop,
you can also place orders directly through our website

www.tempus-publishing.com